Crossing Paths on Television

Crossing Paths board get-together.

Copyright© 1998
Florence W. Biros
ISBN 0-936369-99-X
Printed in the USA

Son-Rise Publications
143 Greenfield Road
New Wilmington, PA 16142
1-800-358-0777

Table of Contents

Environmental Exposure 5
Amazing Grace 17
Peace Follows the Storms 25
First Team with Jesus 42
Imprisonment to Empowerment 57
Mission Impossible 64
Missionary Star 72
They Called Me "Hansi" 77
Eternity Assurance 84
Victory In Jesus 90
From Bitter to Better 100
War - Then Peace 114
Freed from Bondage 128
Free Indeed! 136
The Corporate Junky 144
Hurt, Hope and Healing 151
Green Light Means "Go" 156
The Lighthouse - The Joy of Restoration 163
Modern-Day Noah 171
The Provider 179
Lorraine Who? 195
Sweet Inspiration 201
The Transformation 205
New Kidney, New Heart, New Start 209
When Life Throws You A Curve 217
Renewed Commitment 224

Foreword

This Treasury of awesome stories telling of God's love would not have come into being without Jesus. Each testimony in this book was willingly shared by a Christian who loves the Lord. It would not have been possible without Don Reed's vision of having folks share their life before and after Crossing Paths with Jesus on TV, radio, and through books. Crossing Paths is now featured nationally on Sky Angel throughout America.

Our gratitude also goes to Donna & Jim Jackson for their typesetting skills; Judy McKenna for editorial work; to Barbara Michel, Jean Stewart, Hansi, Joyce Titus, Natalie Sizikova, and Jeniece Learned who penned their own and other's stories.

Special special thanks is extended to "Gideon's Army" the title Don Reed, Gene, and Pam Blakeman have given the devoted workers who make Crossing Path's TV, radio, and book ministry possible.

Environmental Exposure

Lucille Orr

When we opened the door to our spacious new home and knew that our long dreamed-of home had come to pass, all five of us were excited. That quintet included my medical doctor husband, me, and our three offspring. Then of course, our most-adored family member, an old English sheep dog, tagged along.

From the first day in those new surroundings, I became ill. At first I suffered from minor flu-like symptoms including a sore throat; and I thought, in all the hectic days of moving, I'd probably been yelling at the kids too much.

When my symptoms gradually grew worse, I found myself having difficulty just trying to breathe. After I'd eaten and on other occasions, I'd have what doctors called an "anaphylactic attack." Then my throat would close so I couldn't get my breath. Plus other symptoms cropped up in my body. When this happened, panic took over until I could get down my prescribed medication which would help.

Yet sometimes these attacks would get so bad that I'd have to go to the hospital for injections. After receiving those shots, I'd be totally exhausted physically and be bedfast anywhere from one day to three weeks. Then it was so difficult to care for my family. I could hardly stay awake, let alone do anything for them.

Since my husband is a family practitioner, he treated my symptoms. When he could see I wasn't improving, he took me to doctors from Ohio all the way to New York. I finally got too sick to travel.

The specialists tried everything they could, but I was allergic to every treatment prescribed by medical science. I couldn't tolerate anything. Instead of getting better, I kept getting worse.

None of the professionals really seemed to know exactly what was wrong with me. After much testing, a clinical ecologist diagnosed my case. He discovered that I was suffering from what they call EI or MCS; EI stands for environmental illness; MCS -multiple chemical sensitivity. The doctor said I was suffering from a toxic overload from all the new chemicals that I was being exposed to in my new home; carpet, wallpaper, paint, varnish, and every new thing are all filled with odors and some outgas for twenty years or more. All those things were overwhelming my body.

My condition became so bad that the doctors decided I had no option but to be confined to only one room in my home. I became a prisoner in my private quarters with an air filter; for no one could come to see me, and I wasn't allowed to go out.

I suddenly became allergic to things I'd been able to tolerate all my life. No longer were only the major chemicals in the new house bothering me, but tiny little doses of chemicals present in my hair spray, shampoo, perfume, even my own clothes bothered me. I became so sensitive to everything that any smell could send me into a bad attack.

My caretakers told me, "The only thing you can do is to avoid chemicals." That's not easy in 20th-century America since chemicals exist in nearly everything we have.

All the things I'd always done from the moment I got up until the minute I went to bed, I couldn't do any more. To exist, I had to change everything I did and everything I used; I couldn't do anything the same. Overwhelming!

The doctors gave me papers and books and lists and

charts telling me all the things I had to do. I was determined to do them because my weight had decreased to only 88 pounds. I could barely stand up. I was very weak.

My physicians said, "We're afraid you're going to die, and you might die very soon."

I couldn't eat except maybe a carrot for a meal since my body was reacting adversely to nearly all the foods in the house.

Even my clothing and bedding had to be changed — no synthetic clothes or sheets and pillowcases - only cotton. Nothing new. No dry cleaning. No gas heat. No fragrances. No food in a can. No food with preservatives. My mind whirled with all the "No's."

"Don't drink anything but distilled water, eat only organic food, avoid gas stations, don't use anything plastic or Teflon™ or anything coated. No sugar. Avoid people."

That prognosis to me didn't mean living, but just trying to exist. All their mandates were overwhelming, but I set out to try. I did as much as I could and managed to get everything they told me all done, but do you know the worst part about it? I was still SICK!

I had my husband buy any books he could on environmental illness and multiple chemical sensitivities. After reading all this, I felt like an expert. I was personally going to change the world and share with people how to live in a toxic-free environment. This knowledge wasn't just for me, but I wanted it to help everyone.

Doctors all over the country heard from me. I even wrote to Oprah, Heraldo, and even the President of the United States. Oprah never answered. Heraldo said he wasn't interested in my story and "the topic isn't too interesting at this time." The President passed my letter on to somebody who passed it on to someone else who in turn got back to me with something like: Yes, we're sorry that there are a lot of people allergic to chemicals today, but there's nothing we can do about it right now.

With all that, I decided I wasn't going to give up. I was

going to keep on trying to find an answer. "Toxic Watch" is a newspaper with a circulation to 14 cities in Ohio, so I contacted them. I contacted Laura Yeomans, who is acutely interested in chemicals and all the information she can gather about them. All the different cities put my story out under different captions. One was, "Toxic Overload Plagues Local Woman." Another said, "Some Folks Suffer From Reactions to Chemicals."

My name and address were included because I belonged to a support group. The response was overwhelming. People who were desperately ill from toxins, not the same exact case as mine, but similar, wrote. They too were frantic for help but could find no answers.

A little yellow sign appeared on my door which said, "My health depends on you. Do not enter." And then the long list of what might cause me problems was listed. You couldn't even come to my house if you'd been near any of the toxins!

No help anywhere! All I wanted was a pill, an operation, anything to make the nightmare go away. Medical science didn't know of anything to make me better.

One day when the rest of the family was in church I turned on the TV. I'd stayed home, fearing I'd have a toxic attack. Dr. Robert Schuller began talking as I sat feeling sorry for myself that Sunday just a few weeks before Christmas. My 14-, 13-, and 8-year-old children had little prospects for a happy holiday either because their mother was confined to her one-room prison.

Encompassed in a web of desolation, I watched for a while, but then a number appeared on the screen 1-714-NEW-HOPE. Those words really caught my attention. HOPE was what I was searching for. Doctors had really tried to help, but they, too, were being overwhelmed by the hopelessness of my situation.

Picking up the phone, I decided not to lose my courage before I finished dialing the number. A wonderful, upbeat prayer-counselor answered. After a brief introduction, the counselor asked, "What specifically do you want me to pray for?"

After I told him of the seemingly hopeless state of my health, he prayed a beautiful prayer with me. He ended with the words, "You will never be the same." After that, he heaved a sigh and added, "I don't know why I said that."

Neither did I! Was his statement good or bad? But then something happened to me. I felt something I'd never felt before. It swept through me like a ripple effect, as a pebble in the water. Perhaps it would be better to describe it as a gentle ocean wave moving through my body, flowing from the top of my head clear down to my feet. It was as if I'd become a new person. I KNEW that I'd received a touch from God. Then I wasn't sure what it was; now I KNOW it was the Holy Spirit.

For the first time since my illness began, I felt as though I had all my thoughts collected and I could make definite decisions. I sensed that we had to move out of our new house. If I did not, I thought I was surely going to die.

The problem was, we had already rented out our old home. We were living in the new house with three children and a sheep dog, we couldn't buy anything too new, so we began to look for a "new old house."

My in-laws invited us to live with them. Bless their hearts. They are dear and lovely people; but it was hard on everyone having five more people crammed into their little house. The dog was in a kennel, so that wasn't a problem, but it was very difficult! We stayed there for four months. During that time I began to feel better, so I was able to venture out once in a while. Still, my husband and I realized more and more our home was built with too many chemicals for me to live there, so we continued our search for an older home.

Finally we located what we thought was a suitable place, and we moved into it. My life was like a roller coaster — a step forward, then two steps back. One minute I was up and feeling pretty good; the next moment I was back down and miserable. Even though I was feeling a little better, I was still suffering from many attacks.

I belonged to an organization called "Heal" whose purpose is to serve those whose health has been adversely affected by environmental exposures. They advertised a company that published a newsletter for safe products. When you're sick and don't know what to do, you call people who have similiar problems on the phone to see what they're doing. A person might give you a little tip to make you feel better, and you try that suggestion to see if it'll help you.

The one thing about environmental illness is, everything affects everyone differently. Experts claim that 15 percent of the population know they have the problem, and there are many more that have it and don't even know it. So many chemicals affect different parts of the body in unusual ways, so through the newsletters we tried to help and encourage each other.

The devastating thing I learned was that NO ONE ever said they got well, but everyone claimed they were still sick and had to live with it. I didn't want to settle for that. I wanted to find an answer.

One day when I was searching through their phone numbers I was led to call someone who lived in Athens, Ohio, the closest place to where I lived. When I phoned this woman named Barbara, she had some good news for me. She was the very first person who I'd ever heard say she was healed of environmental illness. I was all ears while she told her story.

When I asked her what she had done, she seemed to reluctantly say, "I was healed through prayer."

"What?" I asked again, not certain of what she'd said.

"Through prayer" she reiterated rather reluctantly. I was most interested. She told me that many people weren't too interested or couldn't accept what she had to say.

Barbara said, "You don't have to live with it. Jesus wants you well." She told me about the Christian Healing Ministry in Florida. She said, if you will call them and ask them to pray and tell them what your need is, they will not only offer up prayer for you, but they'll put you in touch with a pastor in your area who holds healing services where they lay hands on the sick and anoint them with oil.

All that was new to me. The church I attended while I was growing up only laid hands on the people who were dying. I'd joined a Presbyterian church when I'd married my husband, and I never saw them do anything like that.

But then dear Barbara began sharing scriptures with me. James 5:14-15 says, *"Is any sick among you? Let him call for the elders of the church; and let them pray over him, anointing him with oil in the name of the Lord! And the prayer of faith shall save the sick, and the Lord shall raise him up; and if he has committed sins, they shall be forgiven him."* (KJV)

After that initial time she continued to call and share scriptures and uplift and pray for me. Barbara shared biblical things that I didn't even know existed before.

Such insight began to excite me. She was telling me about healing services, and it was right there in the Bible! It interested me so much that I began to search through the scriptures. I'd always prayed and gone to church and I'd done all the things that religious people do — sing the songs and say the prayers. I'd taught Sunday School, but God was always Somebody way up there, and I was somebody way down here.

Whenever I tried to read through the Bible, I'd come to all the "begats" which listed all the people's names in the Old Testament and decided it was a nice old history book and I'd put it away.

Suddenly I had a change of heart, having a deep desire to know what else was in there. Scriptures started coming alive. One that really touched my heart was Matthew 7:7 *"Ask and it shall be given unto you."* Not <u>might</u>, but <u>shall</u>! It was amazing how many times I needed an answer, then opened the Bible and there it was! My yearning for His Word continued to grow. *"Seek and ye shall find; knock and it shall be opened unto you (8). For everyone that asketh receiveth; and he that seeketh findeth; and to him that knocketh; it shall be opened."*

Reading the Bible became exciting, for that was something I could do. I was so sick that I couldn't even talk on the phone anymore because I was allergic to the plastic. We had to send away for cotton covers to put over the phone. I couldn't write letters because I was allergic to the ink. Pencil marks didn't show up too well.

I was allergic to electricity, but God showed me what I should do. When I phoned the Christian Healing Ministry in Florida that Barbara had told me about, I asked just as the Bible told me to do, "Is there someone in my area who holds healing services?"

They gave me the name of Pastor Don Bartow in Canton, Ohio, who holds such services. Since he lives about an hour away from me and I couldn't physically manage to go all the way there, I called and asked Pastor Bartow to pray for me.

He did, then invited me to come to a Wednesday night healing service.(They were on Wednesdays then, but now they are held on Tuesdays). I'd been on the down side of my roller coaster ride and had been confined to my home for nearly three months, a restriction my doctors had made.

I assured him, "I'll be there as soon as I'm able to travel no matter how far away you are." I used those three months to learn all I could about a healing ministry by reading God's Word. In the scriptures I was fascinated by the miracles of Jesus, but what I didn't know then is that those miracles are still present today! Jesus is alive and is The Healer even today!

I also consumed other books - "Healing Everywhere", "Jesus Wants You Well"—Kenneth Hagin's books and Pastor Bartow's handbook. My own church had taught me about Jesus and about God but nothing about the works of the Holy Spirit. These books taught me about principles in the Bible that I didn't understand and also taught me how to apply them to my everyday life.

C.S. Lovett's "Jesus Wants You Well" gave me four steps

that I could do. Again, I was excited. There's something about us humans that wants to do something concrete and take over and feel like we are accomplishing something.

Here are the four steps he says we should do:

1. Picture the part of the body that is affected in perfect condition.

2. Picture yourself doing something you can't do now, but you expect to do when you are better.

3. Call or visit your doctor. Since my doctor was in New York, I planned to phone her one day and say "I'm healed."

4. I was to give my testimony in my PRESBYTERIAN church. That was most difficult to imagine.

Suddenly I had a new awareness of my problem. I pictured two mountains - one small; one huge. Compare them to your problem - which size fits your situation? Which one fits your God?

I'd had it backwards. My problem loomed so huge in my mind, but I came to realize that there's no problem too big for God! No mountain is bigger than He is!

I finally was ready to let go and let God! I was going to give the rest of my life to Jesus and put Him in control. I was going to let Him - the resurrected Christ - restore my life and make me whole.

I began to put everything I read into action. When my three months of confinement were up - can you guess where I went? I went to Westminster Presbyterian Church for Pastor Bartow's Healing Service in Canton.

On the way there in the car, everything smelled so bad that I had to put a wet wash cloth over my face because of the road fumes and truck exhaust.

Do you recall the woman with the issue of blood in Mark, Chapter 5? Her story and mine were similar. She'd seen many physicians, but her problem hadn't changed; so she was determined to press through the crowd and touch the hem of Jesus' garment and be made whole. I was determined to make my way through the traffic and exhaust fumes and receive my healing. It'd be a snap for God - she had been sick for 12 years; I'd been sick for 2 1/2.

I was excited! I'd prayed and read and I was ready - ready for a miracle! (I couldn't do anything else). When we finally arrived and went into church, everybody smelled - deodorant, soap, hair spray. I even smelled the church. It made me sick. I didn't know what to do, so I went outside. I spent half of my time outside. From experience I knew my symptoms would start small, then become so large that I'd have to go to the hospital. Not wanting that to happen, I'd run outside then back for a short time. I knew Pastor Bartow was sharing some great miracles, but I didn't hear enough because I kept leaving to go outside. The air was getting too cold, so I came in and said to my husband, "Okay, this is it. I can't stay here any more. You have to take me home."

Being the dear, sweet husband he is, he looked at me and said, "No."

I thought, <u>Now what do I do?</u> Matthew 7:7 came to me and I cried out to the Lord, "If healing is for today, and if Your Word is really, really true," - then I got bold and said, "You're going to have to take away these symptoms or I won't be able to stay here."

I'd no sooner finished asking when I received. I was in awe! He'd instantly, if only temporarily, lifted every symptom from my body so that I was able to remain.

When the time came for laying on of hands - I was ready to go! This was the first time I realized that He wasn't way up there, but He was right there in the midst of the crowd. I realized that Jesus cares for each one of us. Such a great, good revelation! It came to me from God and I knew that 'Jesus Is Alive and Heals Today!' This was my calling to heal.

When I went forward, Pastor Bartow laid his hands on me and prayed the prayer of faith. He anointed me with oil, and I reached out and touched the hem of the Lord's garment just as the woman with the issue of blood did. I knew, even though I couldn't see Him, that He was there and I pressed through to receive my healing. When I reached out to touch Him, I experienced God's power in a way that I didn't think possible. (Believing the power of God was being released, I really touched the hem of Pastor Bartow's garment.) He reveals Himself in different ways, but to me a great peace came upon me - the peace that passeth understanding. Unspeakable joy filled my heart. A feeling, as if a warm glow of honey, went through my body; then I felt as though a weight was lifted. My burden was gone.

Although I didn't experience an instantaneous healing, I was ready to go on. I KNEW that I KNEW that God had touched me. I'd received the beginning of my gradual healing.

For the next 4½ months I no longer looked at my problem, but looked to MY PROBLEM SOLVER, JESUS. He is my physician.

I went down three more times to healing services (now held at the Total Living Center). Each time God's power became more and more real to me. Once I felt as though I couldn't stand another time. A shock went through my body, the last time it was so strong I fell to the floor, ever so gently! So awesome!

I noticed that my health started to improve during this 4½ months. The attacks were farther and farther apart and fewer and fewer in number. I had to walk by faith and not by sight. In my heart I was believing in my healing.

Some days it did not appear that way, but I'd thank Jesus every day and praise Him. Some days I did that with pain in my body and tears flooding my face. I kept reading, believing, and acting upon God's Word, as if I'd already been healed.

Things started happening. People began to notice I was starting to appear in public again. Then one day when I least expected it, my healing became a reality in my life. May 8, 1991, I received my miracle when I was wonderfully and miraculously healed by the power of God.

When we were preparing to move back into our new home, fear set in. The enemy is always there, trying to rob you of your healing right after you received it. A visit from Pastor Bartow and his prayer to rebuke that fear, which I know is nothing more than false evidence appearing real.

When faith came in, fear left.

Two weeks later we moved back to our new home where the doctor said I could never live again. I chose to believe God's Word and not man's.

In Mark 9:23 is a scripture I hold on to. There Jesus said, *"If you can believe, ALL things are possible to him who believes."* That's all He is asking us to do - BELIEVE!

Remember - In the book I read about healing, it told me four steps to picture in my mind: 1. Every organ in my body being healed; 2. Myself being back in circulation; 3. Calling my doctor. I did that! I phoned my doctor in New York and declared, "I'm healed by the power of God!" She replied, "Did you think of going on the 700 Club? There's people on there who have received divine healings." My answer? "If God wants me there - I'll go!"

4. The last thing was to give my testimony in my church. I thought I'd never get to do that, but I'd pictured that. I went back to church the following Sunday and everyone was shocked to see me there. My pastor said, "I wonder if you would come back in a couple of weeks and give your testimony?"

God's good. I went back and told everyone of God's goodness. Now I'm living an abundant life and I'm serving our Risen Savior!

Hosea 4:6 says, *"My people are destroyed for lack of knowledge."* I was almost destroyed because I did lack knowledge until I thirsted for God's Word.

Proverbs 4:20-22 says, "My son, attend to my Words; incline thine ear into my sayings. Let them not depart from thine eyes; keep them in the midst of thine heart. For they are life unto those that find them and health to all their flesh. Keep thy heart with all diligence, for out of it are the issues of life."

I found the truth and the truth can set you free!

* * * * *

Lucille Orr Ministry, Inc., hopes to help heal and transform lives through Jesus. For information about healing services please call 330-533-1985.

Amazing Grace

Sue Thomas with Amazing Grace

When my parents tucked me into bed that night so long ago, they didn't realize that it would be the first long and silent night of the rest of my life. They had no idea that it was the beginning of many years of anguish, frustration, and ridicule.

I was a typical, normal child until I was eighteen months old. In the early evening I was watching TV with my three older brothers. I ran to the television and turned the volume up full blast. My brother hurried to turn the volume down. I kept turning it up; he kept turning it down. It didn't take Mom and Dad long to come in to find out what all the ruckus was about! Assuming my crankiness was because I was tired, they just put me to bed.

The next morning, I didn't pay any attention to what Mom was saying and was unaffected by sounds. It didn't take long for her to realize that I was oblivious to my surroundings. Concerned, she called a neighbor who was a nurse. After a lot of discussion, I was rushed to the hospital. When the doctors examined me, they turned to my parents and spoke the words that would echo through their minds and hearts for the rest of their lives....

"There's absolutely no hearing there. She is profoundly deaf."

Doctors and educators alike tried to convince my parents that it would be best to put me in a deaf institution. They said I would never be able to learn in a normal fashion; I would have a hard time doing anything, let alone learning to speak. My parents didn't want to send me away. They took a silent vow to do everything possible to help me live in a world without sound.

There have been various people along life's journey that have helped me. The first one that was really instrumental is one I call a "mean old lady." She was my speech therapist. The first day I walked in and saw her face, I knew I was in trouble. Not only was she old, but also she looked awfully mean. I didn't realize that the half-hour session would turn into seven long years. I sat before a mirror watching how she formed her mouth, then I would try to form my lips in the same way. I would put my hand on her throat to feel the vibrations, then I would try to duplicate it. She seemed terribly mean. Why did she seem so? No matter how hard I tried to do what she wanted me to do, it was never good enough. All I ever saw was a frown on her face and her shaking her head. "No, you didn't do it right. Do it again. No. That's not right." Over and over again. I thought she was horrid!

Today I thank God for that mean little old lady, for her life, for her dedication, and for her persistence. If it were not for her, I certainly wouldn't have the ability to speak today.

I had begun my training and therapy at the age of two, which was shortly after my parents discovered my deafness. After seven years, it was no longer beneficial to work with the "mean old lady."

My parents then brought in a voice teacher. I don't sing in any way, but the lessons were to get my voice to fluctuate. This was so I would not speak in a monotone.

After two years of voice training, we brought in an English, dramatic-reading teacher. With her coaching, I would recite poetry; hour after hour I practiced articulation and pronunciation. I've had many years to develop my speech, yet I realize that I still talk funny.

People don't laugh at me now like they did when I was growing up. At the airport, during my travels, people come up and ask, "Where are you from? You really have an accent."

This indicates to me that I talk a bit differently; but I have no doubt that the Lord has given me this particular voice to proclaim His faithfulness. I frequently speak to junior high and senior high school kids. The feedback from the teachers and principals is always the same. They say they've never had an assembly so attentive or so quiet. I know it's the Lord using my "bit different" voice that maintains the kids' attention. God took what was once a tremendous hardship that was the brunt of laughter and ridicule and used the power of faith to create something glorious. I no longer have a problem with the voice God gave me.

The experience reminds me of Romans 8:28, *"All things work together for good for those who love God and are called according to His purpose."*

After getting past "the mean old lady," I wish I could say that my story ended perfectly, but I found out that my journey was becoming more difficult, rather than easier. I went to school. The lessons there were very hard to learn; and way back then, my voice was really funny. The kids laughed at and tormented me.

The number one question I have from kids in schools today is, "Do you still get laughed at?" Or, "What did it feel like to be laughed at?"

I always ask, "How do *you* feel when you get laughed at?" Nobody likes to be laughed at. One thing I can honestly say is that as much as I hated that laughter then, I thank God for it now. Why? Because if I had not suffered the anguish of laughter aimed at me, I wouldn't know the pain others experience when they are made fun of. It taught me something about how to relate to kids today. When I go into elementary schools, my main topic is, "Let's talk about the laughter.... let's talk about the pain that goes with it."

In school, I sat in the front so I could watch my teacher's lips as she asked questions. I never got to answer because all the smart kids behind me raised their hands and gave the answers first. This made me hate school. Those days were filled with taunting laughter and ridicule. Eventually, to get the kids to stop tormenting me, I took matters into my own hands and punched them out on the playground! In their minds, I became a "dummy" because I didn't have the understanding of the questions, let alone the answers to them. My grades became D's and F's.

In looking back, I often wonder if I might not have completely wiped out in that world of silence—if it had not had been for the love and understanding of Jesus Christ.

There were three important things. First, at a very young age, my parents kept telling me, "As long as you put your hand in the hand of Jesus and hold on, He will lead you and guide you through life; and there won't be anything you won't be able to do or become."

Secondly, I had roller-skating. Through my love for skating, I came up against the state champion. I had a coach who believed in me and who worked overtime to help me skate because I couldn't hear the music. Through his ears and commitment, I became the Ohio State Champion.

Thirdly, I had a song. I don't remember what music sounded like, but I have had a mother that loves music. She wanted to pass that love on to me whether I could hear or not. I remember as a little child, she would sit in the rocking chair with me in her lap and my head on her shoulder. As she sang, I could feel the vibrations. If I liked the song particularly well, my hand would creep up so that I could feel all the vibes that I could. It must have been around Christmas time, for one of the first songs that my Mom taught me was Silent Night. As a small child, I didn't understand what the words meant. It was the rhythm that made it a tremendous piece for me.

After I went to the principal's office and got spanked for

punching my taunters, I came back to my desk, looked out the window, and braced my lower lip so I wouldn't cry. Way down deep, I would sing *Silent Night* and find peace. On the bus on my way home from school, I'd look out the window with my nose pressed against the glass so no one would see my tears. Way down deep, I'd be singing *Silent Night*. The peace would come.

After being a champion skater and having all the trophies, as well as having Jesus, you'd think it would be enough for me. It could have been, but in truth I really didn't know Jesus. I had Him in my thoughts and in my heart, and I'd hold on to Him when things were going good. But I had a very strong will as a child. I guess I still have it, to some degree, but God is molding it and shaping it.

At times I would ask Jesus for things; and I would wait and wait for the answer. When it wasn't the answer I wanted, I would go out to get the answer I wanted. This happened a lot when I was in school.

One of the worst things about being deaf and living in a silent world is that a deaf person constantly goes out, but no one can come into that world of silence. Many times I longed for a friend. But who wants to be a friend of a dummy? Who wants to be a friend of someone who talks funny? I never had that friend until I was a freshman in high school. Imagine going all those years without understanding what the word "friendship" meant. The friends I made in high school were the wrong kind. I turned from Jesus to go to those friends because I could see them. I could touch them. But when I let God speak to me, I could hear His still small voice within me.

My high school years were turbulent. It wouldn't be until my junior year that I started taking on another dimension. That happened when I met the second meanest old lady in my life — my typing teacher. She saw something in me that no one else did. She believed that I wasn't a dummy and began working with me one-on-one. Because of her support and influence, I went on to college. It took me almost eight years to graduate, but when I did, I thought I was ready to lick the world! I thought everybody would want to hire me. The problem was — nobody did. Why? I couldn't use the telephone. Why hire someone who couldn't hear? If an employee were on a coffee break and the phone would ring, a deaf person couldn't answer it.

I went back to the speech-therapy center where I had learned to speak. I knocked on the door and asked for a job. I know they felt sorry for me. Why? They hired me when no one else would. I became like a jack-of-all-trades for them, and I appreciated the opportunity they gave me. I was there for only three months because God had different plans for my life.

I had a friend at the hearing and speech center whose son lived in Washington D. C. He had a friend who worked for the federal government. Through these connections, I ended up being hired into the FBI in Washington. By God's grace and God's grace alone, He took a totally deaf person and had me climb the ranks of the FBI. I became an undercover surveillance agent. I would follow the bad guys around, read their lips, then tell the good guys what the bad guys were saying. They even paid me to do it!

After three years of life in the fast lane of Washington, I came to realize there had to be a lot more to life than the Washington scene. I resigned, not realizing the journey on which God was about to take me.

I headed south to begin seminary. It was during my days at seminary that I came to really know the Lord Jesus Christ. I discovered that people can go to church every Sunday and say, "Yes, I believe," and they think they do. I had gone through all the right motions, but it was not until I hit the rock bottom of my life that I went to the Cross. I clung to Jesus with everything I had and ask him to come in and take over.

While I was in seminary, I studied the Scriptures and prayed with about thirty friends. Even though I was present, I wasn't really there. I do okay when I'm with one or two persons because I can easily read their lips. But each person added to the group made my lip-reading job more difficult. Often by the time I discovered who was speaking, the person had said a paragraph and I was lost.

So many times I cried out, "Oh, God, give me my hearing back!"

Every time He said, "No, not yet."

Once again, I went my wayward way. I conjured up a whopper of a lie. I told my seminary friends that I had a terminal disease and that I was dying of cancer. Why would I do that? Because I honestly thought that if they believed me, they would want to spend as much time as possible with me one-on-one. That's exactly what happened. I didn't realize when I told that lie that it would last for seven long months. Nor did I realize when I told the lie to one person, it would reach out to twenty people. It was that lie that brought me to my all-time low.

I was spiritually wasting away. I confessed my lie and went to the Cross and asked Jesus to forgive me and become my Lord and Savior.

Each one of us has a handicap. It doesn't need to be a physical limitation. Without Christ, we are nothing.

When I confessed my sin, I realized that my life had to be totally transformed. The people in seminary taught me about the love and forgiveness of Christ. So many times when I went to chapel, I was feeling so lousy about myself for what I'd done. I would stand outside the chapel doors feeling too unworthy to go inside.

One day the Dean of Women gave me an article to read. It was about the hearing-dog program. I read it but didn't do anything with it.

The next week at church, a little lady about eighty-four came up to me and said, "Sue, I just read this article, and I know it's for you." She handed me the same article! *"Certified Hearing Dogs for the Deaf train dogs to be the ears for a deaf person."* I didn't realize that God had a very precious gift waiting for me.

I went to train with Levi, my first dog. He became a vital part of my ministry. He and I would go into maximum-security prisons. I had one prisoner come up to me and say, "Lady, I haven't seen a dog in nineteen years." Because of my dog, he came to chapel that night to hear my testimony.

Two years ago Levi passed away. It was a very sad time in my life, and I still miss him today. I went back to the world of silence that I'd almost forgotten, but God had another dog waiting for me. The owners of a show dog decided to put her into the therapy dog program. She was to be trained for a person in a wheelchair; but when they heard about my plight, they transferred from the therapy program to the hearing-dog program.

I asked, "What's her name?"

They said, "Grace."

"Grace? No kidding! Everywhere I speak, she'll be known as Amazing Grace." She has to earn her title, though. It's not a free gift from God like our salvation!

She has done her job very well. She has won over the hearts of the "bullies." She is not just a conversation piece; she is a valuable extension of my ministry. When someone knocks on my door, she finds me and lets me know. When my alarm clock goes off in the morning, she wakes me up. She's foolproof! Through my days as well as through my long silent nights, she has indeed become "Amazing Grace."

Today Grace and I travel the world together sharing our story and the message of hope and God's love. Only God could envision a totally deaf child later in life speaking to thousands and sharing His hope. Whatever challenge you are facing today, rest assured that God is in control, and that He has enough "Amazing Grace" for your situation too!

* * * * *

If you are interested in obtaining Sue Thomas' life story in a 298 page hard cover book entitled *Silent Night*, please send $19.95 plus $3 shipping and handling to:

Sue Thomas
PO Box 9273, Boardman, OH 44513

Peace Follows the Storms

Denise Scott

I was born and raised in a small town in Northeastern Ohio. As the fifth child in a family with six children, I accepted the Lord at an early age. My teen years were spent in the church and how I loved to play the piano and sing contemporary Christian music there! But around the age of 16, no one could have told me that my life was about to change literally overnight.

It was the fall of 1980, and I was excited about going to my youth group meeting that evening where we were planning to prepare Thanksgiving baskets to give to the needy. The morning air had a snappy chill to it as we rushed to prepare for the holiday. But it was on that day that I told my mom about some strange symptoms I was having. She decided that we should visit the doctor. We did, and he indicated that I should have a D & C done. "But, Mom," I protested, "I can't do that. I've got to help make the baskets at church tonight. Can't I be admitted tomorrow? I just can't go to the hospital today." But no matter how I protested, to my great displeasure, I was told by my mother and the doctor that I HAD to go in.

Now, if there was anything that I hated, it was the hospital. I disliked the smell of a hospital, and I was especially fearful of needles. The thought of having a surgical procedure made me very uncomfortable. The next day in the hospital, I was given anesthesia. The procedure was performed, and I woke up somewhat disoriented in the recovery room. I remember hearing the doctor saying something about my kidneys being so bad that I might possibly need a transplant. Transplant! I thought, *oh, I just couldn't have heard him right.* Later when my parents entered the room, I asked them, "What is this about a kidney transplant?" I was hoping that it was just a bad dream after being sedated. But my parents words sounded clear. I wasn't prepared for their answer. " Denise, they want you to go to Cleveland Clinic for more tests." Everything was happening so fast. That was on Friday. On Tuesday my parents drove me to Cleveland where they admitted me. Through the day they performed dozens of tests. Later that same day the doctor came to me and said that my kidneys were working only one percent, if that, and that I would have to begin dialysis the next day. At that moment I felt as if I had been tossed into a well of quick sand. The events of the last few days were pulling me farther and farther downward with each test result — covering me, smothering the very breath in me. "DIALYSIS!" I began to plead, "Can't I just have a transplant instead?"

The answer was quick from the doctor. "Denise, you're too ill to have a transplant now. You'll have to go on dialysis first."

The news was so staggering for me. I was Shocked! My parents and the nurses tried to comfort me, but I would only roll over in the bed. I pulled myself inside a shell and just stared at the wall, refusing to speak. The tears welled up in my eyes. I couldn't understand. I just couldn't believe it. I remember lying in the hospital looking out the window in my room to the evening sky talking to my Savior, "Lord, if you're going to take me, I know where I'm going." That night impacted me so much because of the fear that encompassed me; I will never forget it. My only understanding of dialysis was from an uncle. Even though his condition had nothing to do with mine, I remember years before of my parents asking me to pray for him because the medical personnel had so much trouble hooking him up to the machine.

The nurse pushed me down the corridor to the dialysis room. My mother and father walked beside us. As the door opened, they began to follow me inside. But the nurse said, "Your parents can't go in there with you." Panic began to take me. I began to pray. It seemed that I was truly alone. I knew that this was a road that only God could accompany me on. So my mother and father were seated outside while I went in to be hooked to the machine. I began to cry inwardly saying, "Come on, Lord, you can change all this! You have all power. You can heal me. I don't need to go into that room. God, I believe in Your power to heal." And yet my situation never changed. Anger swept through me at times, but fear began to penetrate my heart so deeply that I couldn't get it out of my mind.

My parents prayed for me, with my dad quoting scripture from II Timothy 1:7: *"For God hath not given us the spirit of fear; but of power, and of love, and of a sound mind."* It's one thing to quote those verses, but another thing to have it so deeply in your heart that it calms you when you are faced with uncertainty. What a blessing His Word is. The Bible says that He sent His Word, and His Word healed them. My healing at that point was not physical, but His Word began to heal me emotionally. Inside the room an intern hooked me up to the machine, but he had a difficult time connecting me to it. Finally they let my parents in, and we began to talk. But suddenly something was wrong!! The intern made my parents leave quickly, and then I blacked out. It was at that time that I had that tunnel experience that people talk about, hanging somewhere between Heaven and Earth, leaving to be with the Lord. The initial dialysis treatment had been a tremendous shock to my system, almost more than my body would tolerate. But minutes later I was OK. Thank God.

That began three years of treatments. Throughout that time, God was my Shepherd; God was my help in time of need. For only He was capable of going with me into every experience that I would face. During those long, tiring months, the Enemy tried to take my life - and my mom's. I remember times when we were returning from dialysis treatments, which was an hour-and-a half away from our home in Columbiana. So often I slept in the car on the way home because the treatments were physically draining. My mother, who was always so faithful, would drive; but she was almost as exhausted as I was. Many times I would wake up just as the car was drifting toward the edge of the highway and shout, "Mom, wake up you're going off the road!" Yet He kept us safe. His mercy is everlasting.

The doctors had a hard time getting needles into my arms. Before going to work each morning, my dad would often pray with me that they wouldn't have trouble getting me on the machine. I can envision my mother as she paced the hall praying while they attempted to get the needles in my arm. My life was far removed from the bouncy teenager that I was. I was so ill; I had to lie on the couch or in bed most of the time. The doctors didn't like to give me blood transfusions because they created more antibodies, making it more difficult to match me for a transplant. A few times the doctor made an exception. One was when I graduated from high school. I was determined to walk across the platform and accept my high school diploma. They agreed to give me three blood transfusions so I could walk on my own strength. And I did. The Lord was somehow always merciful. During the three years that I received dialysis, my family was all tested to see if they could donate a kidney, but none of them matched. "Sorry, you'll have to wait for a cadaver," the doctors said - which meant I had to wait for someone to die to get a kidney.

During that long waiting time I know God was working on my fears — the fear of the known — and fear of the unknown. I believe now that the reason that I could not get that transplant was because I had too much fear in my life, and He was helping me work it out. In December of 1983 at a Full Gospel Businessman's Fellowship Dinner, I heard a speaker say, "No matter how often you go forward for a healing, you are never to quit. Keep going if you need a touch in your life." Those words witnessed to my spirit, and that night God released me! I knew as I left that building that something was different. Physically, I was the same; but I know that the message gripped my heart so deeply that I gave up the fear. I could see beyond my seemingly hopeless situation, and I truly grasped that I would and could have a transplant. I could face the unforseen. Every night after that I expected a call saying it was my turn. One night about thirty days later the call came, the one I'd waited for. They had the kidney labeled for me. A precious family was giving me life unselfishly through the death of their loved one. How grateful I am to the family that cared enough to give me life during their time of grief! I do not know their names, but I pray the Lord's blessing upon them for such a sacrifice. The transplant went well, and I rejoiced and praised the Lord that I finally had the opportunity to have a normal life. My new kidney worked so well that I began working for the Department of Human Services. My life was so free compared to the years when I was chained to the dialysis machine. What a difference!

My life was back on track again. The opportunities were limitless before me. During that time I sang and played the piano for many weddings. Sometimes I would play for three weddings during one day, going from one to another. It was all so beautiful; I loved the whole ambiance of the ceremony. But I also felt very lonely. Now, please don't get me wrong. I was thankful for the blessing of health that the Lord was providing. But there was just that loneliness and my longing to be in a God-anointed relationship. I knew that it would take someone special to be my husband. But I also had faith and knew that God had that someone waiting. As I would look at the sanctuary filled with flowers, the bride would make her way down the aisle. Those experiences were very emotional for me. Would it ever be my turn to be married? I couldn't help but wonder if any man would ever want to marry me because of my physical limitations. I knew it would take a very special man to want to be my husband.

I often prayed for this man, but I recall once I fasted and prayed for three days and three nights for that specific reason, which can be more difficult for someone on major medications. I asked the Lord to bring me the desire of my heart — someone with whom I could sing; someone with whom I could pray, so that we could touch hurting people with the love of Jesus and bring people to the saving knowledge of His love, mercy, and grace. How often I was part of a crowd, and yet so alone. At times I knew I wasn't invited to parties because I was single. Those were very hurtful times. People would tell me, "Let God be your husband." I did. He sustained me through that difficult period, but still I never ceased praying for that very special person.

The Bible says in Psalms 37:4 *"Delight thyself also in the Lord and He shall give you the desires of thine heart."* In 1990 the Lord prompted me to go to California. My brother lived there, and after a visit with him, I felt that I was to move. This was difficult because of the close ties I had with my family and the ministry which I was involved in at our church. Mom and Dad had been so faithful to love and uphold me through my illnesses and loneliness that it was most difficult to let go and leave them.

Yet I moved to Sacramento. Within three months I was dating a man, who, on top of loving the Lord and having a beautiful voice, was to become my husband. Our circumstances just seem to work out right when our steps are ordered by the Lord. Our first date was to Yosemite and from then on, love blossomed. Roger and I talked before our marriage and decided that we should not try to have children because of my physical condition. And we were both OK with that. And so, on February 15, 1992, (I will never forget the day), it was my turn to walk down the aisle. I knew that my choice was the Lord's choice, too. Such a glorious day!

Eleven months later, to our great surprise, "we" got pregnant! What an incredible thing! I thought that my joy was full in finding marriage, but now a baby? I was awestruck at God's plans. However, because of the risk of losing my kidney or even my life, and also the possibility of heart problems or other major complications to the baby, we were told that I should have an abortion. Any mental picture of me lying in bed in a hospital room and having someone take my child and discard it as garbage was more than my mind could fathom. No way could I abort this child!

When I was about eighteen weeks pregnant, we were at the doctor's office preparing to have a sonogram for the first time. My obstetrician looked at my husband and said, "Now I know that we have asked you to make a decision concerning continuing this pregnancy. If seeing the fetus move about on the screen makes this decision too difficult for you, then just turn your head and look away."

Roger, amazed, simply replied, "It's still a child with a beating heart, whether I look or not. Looking away does not change the presence of life inside." I think that was the day the doctors knew that I would not consider losing our baby. The doctors told us, and we knew all-too-well, that we would have to trust in the Lord to take care of our infant and me.

The Bible says in Psalms 139 verses 15, 16 and 17: *"You were there while I was being formed in utter seclusion; You saw me before I was born and scheduled each day of my life before I began to breathe. Every day was recorded in your book. How precious it is, Lord, to realize that You are thinking about me constantly; I can't even count how many times a day Your thoughts turn toward me. And when I waken in the morning, You are still thinking of me."*

God knew my baby in my womb and was merciful to me all during the pregnancy. I was on bed rest from May to September because of high blood pressure and had to stay on my left side the entire time. When it came time to deliver the baby, he was delivered by Cesarean section. The surgery went well, and we became the proud parents of a handsome baby boy named Nathaniel Ryan Scott. Oh, what joy!

As he was being delivered, the doctor proclaimed, "Well, here is our miracle baby!" And I said "Amen" to that!

Another physical problem developed for me a day or two after the delivery. I had lost only a small amount of blood during the surgery, and yet the doctors said that I was very low on blood. Again Satan came against me. The Bible says, *"The thief comes only to steal and kill and destroy; I have come that they may have life, and have it to the full."* God wants us to have life. But the Enemy wants to take it.

We worked through that situation with blood transfusions. I was very sick and it was scary — I had a newborn. So amazing. One evening my husband would take Nathan home from the hospital without his Mama. I could see that he so wanted both of us to come home. Thank God for a caring husband who walked with me through that trying time. I returned to my room where now the empty crib stood. But I knew that I was not well enough to go home. Now, the lab tests were showing something awry. It seemed that something might be happening to the transplanted kidney. Our delight changed to concern as my husband and I wondered if I was about to face dialysis again.

We prayed and prayed that God would touch my kidney. There were times when Roger would come to my hospital room around 4:00 or 5:00 a.m. I still smile because somehow we would find room in that small hospital bed for both of us. He'd put his arms around me, and we would begin to pray and sing songs of praise and worship to the Lord together. We knew that the Lord WOULD make a path through this seemingly impossible situation.

In the flesh we kept wondering why He would bring us through a successful pregnancy and delivery, and then shortly afterwards have me begin to have problems all over again two days after my healthy baby was born. How could He allow my kidney to fail and leave me with the prospect of facing dialysis once more when I'd thought that ordeal was all over for me?

Heartsick, I realized I had to face yet another challenge.

The doctors couldn't understand why I was so anemic that I could hardly lift my head to speak. One day the kidney doctor came into the room and announced that he thought that the doctors wanted to perform a biopsy on my kidney. As the doctor left the room, he indicated that he would return in the morning to reconsider.

My mind went back to the first days of dialysis and the fear I'd experienced. How I yearned to be with my child when he learned to walk, to talk, to lose his first tooth, to be there for his first day at school. It seemed that I was at a crossroad, crossing the path where fear and faith meet. "Lord," I cried inwardly, "please let me live!" The doctor left the room, and Roger and I began to think about the coming day and what it would bring.

Roger left my room to drive home. It was about seven that Sunday evening. Exhausted and drained from the emotional and physical trauma of the preceeding months and especially the events of this day, Roger looked across the freeway and could see several churches, where they were still holding evening services. He talked to his Loving Heavenly Father as he went by, "Lord, you know we'd both be in church tonight if we could. What good-what glory to You-can this situation possibly bring? "

Needing gas, he pulled into a filling station. Deep in thought, suddenly he heard a voice over his shoulder say, "Excuse me, sir, but our car is broken down, and we were wondering if you could give us a ride." Roger glanced up and saw that two Russian teenagers were asking him for a way home. His usual answer would have been "no" as most people are afraid to give anyone a ride anymore, even for a short distance. Yet there was something about those boys that made him ask where they were going.

The two young men said that they'd been on their way to church; but their car had broken down, and they had no way home. As tired and frazzled as my husband was from the pressures of that day, the word "church" got his attention. He agreed to take them to their destination.

Glancing at his passengers as they piled in the back seat, Roger drove for a few miles in silence. "Are you boys Christians?" Roger asked.

Their reply was definite, " Praise the Lord! Yes, we are. Are you a Christian?" My husband assured them that he was.

The young men directed him to the other side of town. As Roger drove them the many miles to where they said they lived, he said, "Boys, I'd like to ask you for a favor. My wife has just delivered a baby boy who we have named Nathaniel which means "gift of God." But it seems that now, only a few days later, her kidney might be failing. Will you pray for her as the doctors do a test tomorrow, and possibly a biopsy?"

Roger said that as he looked into the rear view mirror, he felt the power of God rush into the car. The blue eyes of the smaller Russian boy seemed to glow like coals of fire as he said firmly, "Oh, yes, we will pray for your wife, but I tell you what you have to do. You must go, and get the oil, and anoint her, and pray for her, and Jesus WILL heal your wife."

My husband realized that a week overburdened with challenges had robbed us of the time to regroup and speak peace into this chaotic circumstance. Isn't it wonderful to have the calming words of scripture to bring peace in those kinds of troubled times? We get so pre-occupied that we are diverted from acting upon the basic concepts of the Bible. Yet, here, a Russian teenage stranger lit a spark of hope in such a dark, seemingly hopeless situation.

As the boys left the car at their destination, Roger turned to say goodbye. He looked across the street, but they were gone! We believe that God used those two young Russians to minister to my husband directly. Were they angels? We don't know, but we are certain that the Lord sent them to give hope to us at a time when we could see nothing but trouble ahead.

Roger came to the hospital early that next morning. He

slipped into my bed again. I could feel him snuggle up against me. Without either of us speaking, he held me in the shadows of dusk. And then in that room with only the two of us, my husband began to softly, slowly sing. We'd sung together doing concerts at churches, but this concert was not directed to a congregation, but to a host of witnesses heavenward — yes, to even God Himself.

I joined him in singing softly that dear song written by Don Moen, "God will make a way where there seems to be no way." This song had been written by a man, who in the face of adversity, was proclaiming his trust in God. We had sung this song together to so many hurting people. And now this song was ministering to our own broken selves — a young couple, new parents. Clinging to each other, clinging to God. We wonder now what the hospital staff thought as they heard the two of us worshipping the Lord. Yes, even a hospital room can become a house of worship. A place of peace. Then Roger took the oil and anointed me as he prayed for my kidney function. He then told me the story of the two Russian boys and how they had reminded him of the simple command of Christ. For nine months we had prayed fervently for my pregnancy and the baby boy within my body, and now we were being challenged to pray further. The battle was not over! My husband performed what The Word had told us to do, to pray the prayer of faith and anoint the sick with oil. And now it was up to God to take care of the rest!

At the top floor of the hospital was an observation room which looked down on the city of Sacramento. My mind went back to the night before when Roger and I found our way up there. We sat together and looked off into the distance where we could see the lights on the river below. The California State Fair was in full swing. The ferris wheel was circling high in the sky. Colorful neon lights flashing, shades of pink, blue and gold, illuminated the people who were out there enjoying life. There we were, in the solitude of this observation room, looking down on all the action, just watching, waiting.

As the sun arose, I realized that the doctor would return soon for the decision of whether to perform the biopsy or not. Roger rose to leave for work. I found myself walking with him to the door. I had the strength! Once there, I told my husband, "Wait a minute. I'll walk you to the elevator."

In my hospital gown, we walked arm and arm past the nurses' station to the elevator. As the door opened, Roger reached out to give me a good-bye hug, but I had other plans instead. I stepped inside the elevator with him and eagerly said, "I'll go down with you." On the first floor he got out. To his surprise — so did I!

We walked toward the main doors of the hospital, arm in arm. Turning to my husband, I whispered: "I'll walk you to the car." At the main doors of the hospital, Roger stopped and looked into my eyes. He could see how much I wanted to go with him, but we both knew it was impossible.

With tears in his eyes he held me and whispered, "I'll be back in a few hours, dear." And I watched him leave to go to work.

I returned to my room to await the decision of the doctors. Later that morning the doctors decided that a biopsy was necessary.

And so the biopsy was done that day, and the doctors found only signs of partial rejection which they thought I might have had even before I got pregnant. That was really a praise because it proved that there were no signs of immediate rejection. But I want you to know that if that biopsy had shown otherwise, the Lord still would have been with me, and He would have walked with me down that road. My health problems continued as the medication took its toll on my body. But I know that God is faithful to complete that perfect work in me that will make me be everything that He would have me become.

In May, 1995 I would need another transplant. My first transplant lasted eleven years, with the average non-related kidney lasting from six to seven years. I had been blessed with longevity. Now my whole family was tested once more to see if there would be a match. One of my brothers did. Steve very unselfishly offered me one of his kidneys so that I could have another chance at life through the help of the Lord. What a blessing his gift gave me physically, and what a great bond it created between me and my brother!

About the time of my second transplant, I began to have a breathing problem; but no one had any idea what it was. Minor at that time, it seemed better during the day; but I'd wake up at night because my breathing awakened me. I would use a second pillow and that would help for a while, but then I began having difficulty most of the day and night. Every night when I put my head back to go to sleep, I'd wake up immediately because I had difficulty getting enough air. Some nights I only had one or two hours rest because I couldn't breathe. Emergency room visits became frequent. No one could come up with a diagnosis until the doctors finally told me that it was all in my head, and I needed to see a psychiatrist! I KNEW that it was NOT in my head! After 16 years of illness, I was able to figure out when my body was giving me signals that something was very wrong. But, who was going to help me? Over and over I cried, "Please, Lord, help me! I need to breathe. I need for You to intervene."

We got no answers. Only silence. I remember driving down the road with the cellular phone in the car beside me in case I had an emergency with my breathing. One day I was going down the road praying, "Please, Lord, please! Show us what the problem is with this breathing. I need Your help. I need Your help again." I began to just listen in the quiet of my car. The Holy Spirit, the Comforter, began to speak to my heart. *"Weeping may remain for a night, but joy cometh in the morning."* He also said, *"Your mourning will turn to dancing again."* With those two scriptures, I knew that God was speaking peace into my heart, saying: "Denise, right now your joy may not be full, but your tears will turn into joy." I held on to those scriptures like a newborn clings to his mama. The Lord gave me hope by placing those scriptures in my heart. There may be times, as we have had, that no hope existed except for the Bible verses He has given us. Answers to prayer come, but often we have to wait. There may not be another shoulder to cry on here on this earth, but there is that still, small voice speaking to you about your needs. That is the thing you must cling to because it is the voice of Jesus! I KNEW the LORD HIMSELF had given those words to me directly, and I could hide them on the inside of my mind and heart.

About two years went by, and we decided that we should try a teaching hospital out of our area. So we went to the Stanford Medical Center where they were able to diagnose my problem in a period of about twenty minutes. I had been on steroids for about 13 years as an anti-rejection drug. The steroids caused a muscle in my stomach to stop working and was causing me major problems. Again I had to go for surgery. The last time I'd had surgery, previous to that, was during my second transplant. At the end of the transplant, I wouldn't wake up. The doctors asked Roger and my parents, "Has she ever had a hard time waking up from surgery?" To this they replied, "No." My husband said it was a very uneasy and scary time for them and the doctors as well.

Finally, after about two hours, I woke up; but they tested me and determined that I lacked a chemical that the liver produces that would help me wake up after anesthesia. So they would have to use a different medication after any surgery to wake me up again. Naturally, that made me a little more apprehensive about anesthesia in any further operations.

I remember sitting on the bed in a motel in San Francisco before the surgery and praying, "God, I need Your strength. I need You to help me. I need Your help again. I need You to walk with me right now." As I sat there, I opened my Bible to look up the word "peace." I read a few scriptures — Isaiah 26:3, *"Thou will keep him in perfect peace whose mind is stayed on Thee."* When I came to Psalms 4, verse 8, I read, *"I will both lay me down in peace, and sleep: for thou, Lord, only makest me dwell in safety."* As I took those words into my soul, I knew that was the verse of scripture that the Lord wanted me to take to surgery the next day. I felt the Lord wanted me to memorize that scripture, so I did. I repeated it over and over again.

As I went into the pre-op room where they gave me a shot to relax me, I quoted that blessed scripture over and over again. I woke up from that surgery, safe in the Master's hands.

Yet, again, a severe bleeding problem cropped up during that hospital stay. No one could figure out its source even though they brought the best doctors in for consultation. They saw no signs of unusual blood during the surgery. CAT scans were performed to determine the reason. Those brilliant medical men decided I'd have to go back into surgery, so they could decide where the blood was coming from so that I wouldn't bleed to death. Finally the lab work showed that the bleeding had stopped so that I wouldn't have to go under the knife again. Once more, God kept me, saved me, and loved me through it all.

I don't know what you are going through. It doesn't have to be a physical problem for the Lord to minister to your needs. God is faithful and just to help you. Remember what Romans 8:28 says, *"And we know that all things work together for good to them that love God, to them who are the called according to His purpose."* Remember, what you're going through today is to be for His glory and your good. It may not seem like it right now, but it will later. That's what the Word says. The word is "Yea," and "Amen."

The scripture that I'd like to give you, because it has ministered to me so many times and is so good to hide in your heart is from, Romans 8, verses 37,38 and 39, *"Nay, in all these things we are more than conquerors through Him that loved us. For I am persuaded, that neither death, nor life, nor angels, nor principalities, nor powers, nor things present, nor things to come. Not height, nor depth, nor any other creature, shall be able to separate us from the love of God, which is in Christ Jesus our Lord."* Those verses cover it all!

When you are in a car alone, when you are at home alone, no matter where you are, you need an answer. There's One Person Who has the answer. His name is Jesus! No one can separate you from Him. He wants you to have peace. The Bible says, (KJV) *"My peace I leave with you, My peace I give unto you, not as the world giveth, I give unto you. Let not your heart be troubled; neither let it be afraid."* He loves you and desires to minister to you. I pray that you will begin to hide His Word in your heart so that He can minister to you through His Word.

Roger and I have celebrated nearly seven wedding anniversaries, and God has enabled us to minister to others through song and testimony. God has given us the blessing of watching our son grow into such a loving boy, and seeing him go off to a Christian school. His name "Nathaniel" really does mean "gift of God," and he has been such a tremendous gift to both my husband and to me. God is an awesome God!

I did not share my story to bring myself or our experience into the limelight, but to speak peace to all of you who have "dragons" in your own life, the dragons that bring us to the courtyard of isolation and sorrow. The Bible says that *"God's Word is a lamp unto our feet and a light unto our path."* From experience our family knows that The Word can illuminate even the darkest night. When you feel emptiness inside, or indifference by all who once stood by your side, or your body feels abandoned to sickness, those verses of trusting in God are the foundation and basis of His truths that will see you through the storms of life. My dear friend He is there for you — forever!

Footnote from the Editor: Roger and Denise Scott travel and minister in concert.
Their music is anointed and powerful.

* * * * *

If you would like to contact them you may contact them at :
Potters Clay Ministries
PHONE 916-789-2087 or
E-Mail at RogDen@JPS.NET

Denise, Roger, and Nathaniel Scott

First Team with Jesus

Don Reed

"Don Reed?" the man in the postal uniform inquired when I answered his knock at the door of the office of my thirty-five unit motel.

"That's me."

"Sign here."

Obediently I scrawled my name across the envelope marked "Certified Mail #25341." Glancing at the postmark, I shuddered.

"Las Vegas!" What I didn't need was another bill to toss on the pile! Tearing open the envelope, I stared down at a free ticket to what I had once considered a "Gambler's Paradise."

That place was no longer "Paradise" to me. Along with my local gambling, the western city with its fountains of booze, flashing lights, half-dressed show girls, and my five-to-ten-thousand-dollar nightly losses had been my ultimate downfall.

My family, my businesses, my health were all falling apart because of my gambling and alcohol addiction; but I couldn't stop the merry-go-round I'd been whirling around on long enough to pull my wits together and get off. I couldn't resist any chance to gamble or drink, and I couldn't figure out how I had reached that state. It had all come about so gradually — I hadn't realized that it was happening.

I'd enjoyed the lime-light ever since I was a baby. Upon

my arrival at the William Reed household in New Castle, PA in the year 1931, I was welcomed by eight older sisters and one older brother who all took turns pampering me. Two years before another baby boy — my brother Georgie — had died, and I became the family's new fair-haired boy until my brother Merle, the family's last child, arrived.

Of necessity, my mom kept a tight ship. Everything was always in order before we sat down to eat — or we didn't get to eat!

Putting food on the table for all of us was an enormous problem — not only for Mom who had to prepare the food for such a mob, but also for my dad who had to earn the money to buy it. My younger years were post-depression ones, and Dad was lucky to have a job as a street car conductor who earned sixty dollars a week.

I worried every time I heard my parents squabble over money. Many a night I lay awake with insecure thoughts tugging at me. Over and over I wondered, "What if Daddy gets sick and can't work or what if he gets laid off?"

Sometimes when I was in my teens, I retreated to a dark room and took my frustrations out on a dirty book and let demonic thoughts captivate my mind.

There was no "security blanket" for me to cling to then — I never heard any special emphasis put on God or faith although my mother often sang "Jesus Loves Me" and Dad would pick up his guitar and strum while he sang the words to "The Old Rugged Cross." But Jesus was not real to me in any way then. His birth and death were both like something from a fairy tale.

I didn't have Him in my life to any extent, nor did I care to. What I wanted most were things. We didn't have much as kids, so envy was something I had more than my share of. I dreamed of the big cars, the beautiful wife, the elaborate house, the splashy clothes that I saw other people had and vowed that I would have them when I was older. Poverty — even though ours was wrapped in cleanliness and respectability — was not for me!

But in junior high I was sure I found my niche in life and saw that all the possessions I ever craved — glory, fame, prestige — could all be mine if I worked hard. I found basketball was my thing, and I gave it my all.

In high school I sat back and smiled smugly at headlines on the sport page which made such claims as "Miracle Player Don Reed Ties Entire Opposing Team's Score!" In one game as a sophomore, I scored six points in the last minute — giving New Castle an upset victory over mighty Farrell — for years the top team in our WPIAL League.

Many scholarships were offered to me before I even entered my senior year, and I was sure I could become a pro and that the life style I sought after could be mine!

I gloried in the admiration of the fans — especially the squeals and shrieks I heard from girls as I sank basket after basket during the heat of a game. Aside from my sports accomplishments, I enjoyed being called "lover" as much as anything. No one could dispute the fact that I had what is commonly called a "swelled head!"

Grover Washabaugh, the head mentor of the Westminster Titans of nearby New Wilmington, PA, tried to woo me into his camp for my college years. I visited his campus and was much impressed by the scenery, the curriculum, the nearness to home, Grover Washabaugh himself — but most of all — the pretty girls!

My last year in high school, I decided not to sit by on the sidelines during football season. I went out for that sport, too, because I simply could not stand to be a spectator and barely noticed.

What a nightmare that turned into! After a hard tackle, I fell to the ground. The pain! My knee hurt so much that I wanted to vomit. I was half-carried off the field. How disgusting. The season had hardly begun!

Everyone clapped — for my valor I guess — but that was one time the applause didn't turn my head. I just plain hurt too much to care. The injury was so serious the doctors had to remove some of the cartilage. I was told, "Stay off that leg if you want to have it heal completely."

Basketball practice started, and no doctor was going to bench me! I practiced and worked out and did my best to pretend that gnawing pain wasn't there, but try as I might to forget its presence — it was always with me.

Once the season was started, I began looking forward to the Ellwood City game because teammates and fans were laying bets that I could top the scoring record I'd made the year before when I'd outscored that whole team by myself.

From the toss-up on, I found the Ellwood quintet hadn't forgotten, either. They all seemed to be out to get me — all five of them kept breathing down my neck. One guard never moved from my side.

Finally, deliberately or not, he floored me. I lay there — again grimacing with the agonizing pain. My leg problem was so severe afterwards that my whole senior year scoring record was botched up.

I became apprehensive about my college career because Grover Washabaugh was such a fine guy, and I didn't want to let him down. In no way did I want to lessen the chances for his Westminster Titans to come out on top, so I tried to turn down my scholarship. But that fine man wouldn't renege on his offer, and I wound up playing for Westminster until my junior year when I decided to drop out of college. There was no way I could stand being benched, but my leg was bothering me so much that I wasn't able to stand up to the pressure of a whole game. Grover had no choice but to keep me in reserve.

No job, no degree — what could I do? I'd deliberately put myself out in left field when I left school, so I was sure pleased when I landed a job as a draftsman for Penn Power. While I was working there, I started running around evenings with a friend named Bob Pilch. One night we went to a square dance. While I was standing on the sidelines surveying the scenery, I spied one of the slickest chicks I'd ever seen.

Sauntering over to her, I threw her a straight pitch. "Hi — ever hear of Don Reed — the one who broke all the basketball records?" I was out of high school, out of college, but I was still trying to keep my mental standing as a "star."

Her answer threw me a curve. "Who's that?" My ego was so deflated that it took all the rest of the evening for me to recover and finally admit to her that she was talking to Don Reed in the flesh!

I started courting Donna Heinlen and found she was the only girl I ever tried to date who wouldn't swallow all the bait I tossed her way. The harder she was to get — the more I wanted her.

The more serious I became about her, the more concerned I was about my future. I really didn't have a lot to offer, so I thought, "Why not try the army? They train you to do things."

Twice I tried to enlist; twice I was turned down. Finally I lied about my bum knee and suddenly found myself enroute to Fort Knox, Kentucky.

Talk about a lovesick soldier! Donna had finally confessed that she shared my love just before I enlisted, but I was not prepared for how much of a void her absence left in my life.

Through torturous days of basic training in the heat of the Kentucky sun, I wondered how in the world I had talked myself into that mess! Finally basic was over, and the army moved me to Denver, Colorado. There I got to man a desk.

That was even farther away from Donna than Kentucky had been, and when I thought I could not stand the miles between us anymore — I phoned her. "Will you marry me as soon as you can get here?"

I think my heart stopped temporarily when I heard her answer, "Yes, Don. I will!"

We had a kind of fairy tale wedding as we stood in the chapel on the base and promised, "To love and to cherish until death do us part." That was our vow, and I thought nothing could possibly come between us after that precious ceremony.

We had a honeymoon existence in a cottage at the base

of Pike's Peak until the night when it turned into a nightmare. All of a sudden there were flames, and Donna and I stood helplessly by as all our belongings and dreams went up in smoke. All we had left were the clothes we wore and a smidgeon of personal things she had managed to rescue.

When we learned that Donna was pregnant, we decided it would be best for her if she went home to stay. I knew in my heart that she would be better off back home, but I was a lonely guy. When Uncle Sam's officer called me in and asked, "Don, would you like to be discharged and go home early?" — I went bananas with joy!

My heart soared as the train took me closer to Donna and our child-to-be. A month after my arrival home, I found myself racing the stork to the hospital. Standing beside my wife's bed a short time later, I looked down at my Donna and our first son. "There's you and me and Donnie," I whispered hoarsely. Surely nothing could ever happen that could dissolve that marvelous threesome.

Boy, did I want to do things for my family! With the help of the GI Bill, I resumed my studies with the intention of earning a degree in accounting at Youngstown State University. (Then known as Youngstown College.)

Robert Mort and Associates in Sharon offered me a job, and things started looking like "blue skies and smooth sailing" were ahead of us. I began entertaining clients and found a whole new ball game to play — not basketball, but a thrilling game of wining and dining customers. I was on a new ego trip!

My Donna was not impressed. I was staying out nights with a drink in one hand and poker cards in the other. "You have to socialize to get ahead in this business!" I protested to Donna when she complained to me about my long hours of "entertaining clients."

My nights "out with the boys" turned into continuous drinking and carousing escapades. We had a new home, and Donna objected violently about her nights home alone with Donnie.

"After all," I told her, "I'm just building up business acquaintances so that someday I can have a firm of my own. Do you think I'm doing it just for me?"

That was my argument — even if it was a weak one. I never admitted to her that business was seldom mentioned during my weekend escapades. No woman was going to run my life!

My poker games often ran from Friday night to Monday morning, and I got weaker by each weekend. Sometimes I had to rest up all week just to make it through those three-day drink-athons.

On a Friday night one of my gambling friends arrived with that "just sold an igloo to an Eskimo" look, and I wondered what had given him such a lift. I didn't have to wait long for him to explode with the news, "No poker games next week, you characters! I've got us all on a junket to Vegas!"

"Las Vegas!" I was immediately tantalized. I'd seen pictures of the glitter and the lights and the gambling, and this guy was going to get us free transportation to that glamour spot!

On that trip I got a taste of the big time, and there was no turning back after that. Somehow I was going to make a killing out there that would turn my world into riches!

It never happened. I'd win a little — then lose a lot. After a loss of five or ten thousand in one night, I'd feel sick and think I'd have to stand there and try to get my money back. Those little dice and black jack cards couldn't be against me forever!

One night it got so bad that a pit boss came over to me and asked, "Mr. Reed, don't you think you'd better quit for a while? You must have been shooting craps for twenty hours straight."

I gave in then and went to my room. I lay there and cried out to God for help, but nothing changed. There was an obsession within me that made me go back to the gambling tables again and again.

We had our second son, Doug, and I thought for a short while after his birth that Donna and I could patch our marriage together, but I wasn't really willing to try. I didn't want to give up drinking or the gambling, which had become the biggest part of my life.

Finally I decided to take her along on a trip to Vegas. That move was a disaster from the start. She was beside me the whole time, and I couldn't lie to her then about my winnings or my losses. I'd turned into a compulsive liar along with my other vices because I hadn't wanted her to badger me into quitting, but that night she did. It was obvious that I was only losing — that I had very little chance to get ahead.

I got tanked. Then, mad at my losses and disgusted with her attitude, I wound up nearly choking her! That trip almost put the final axe to our marriage.

I tried to make amends, but Donna stayed aloof and cool. Not long after that trip, I had a chance to fulfill one of my biggest business dreams — the purchase of the Town House Motel in Sharon was within my grasp if I wanted to take it on an article of agreement. Donna was not impressed. "I'll get all the work, and you'll play the part of the town clown!" That was her protest, but I bought it any way.

We worked together to get it going, but Donna's prediction came true. She worked so hard and so long that she at last threw up her hands in disgust and said, "I quit!"

In August of 1974 Donna filed for divorce. A few months before, I'd noticed a drastic change in her — she quit nagging about my escapades. I asked her sarcastically, "What's happened to you?"

Her answer shocked me. "I gave my heart to Jesus. I told Him I just don't care anymore. I'm tired of trying, and if there's anything going to be made of this marriage now — you're going to have to do it."

How I scoffed at her! But things didn't get better — they got worse. Bills kept piling skyward. Vegas demanded immediate payment of my astronomical debts, so my bank loans kept increasing. I found myself caught in a tidal wave of troubles. My business — my motel — my tax practice and other investments — my family — were all falling apart before my eyes, and I was unable to stop the tide.

I tried AA and GA (Gambler's Anonymous) because I'd seen spectacular changes in other people's lives, but neither worked for me. I'm sure I didn't really want to get rid of my vices, but I wanted it to look like I did. Underneath it all — I didn't want my children and wife to leave me.

When I reached the point where I was scared because I realized I couldn't stop gambling and drinking even though I now wanted to, I put myself in the AA Hospital. That night I got scared stiff when the man in the bed next to mine died in the middle of the night. Still — nothing I tried as an external remedy was able to stop my bent toward self-destruction.

And so I reached the day when I sat pondering the future as I sat in my motel office, and the free ticket to Vegas arrived. Words spoken years before by a former pastor of the church where I was a member came to my mind. Rev. Jack Williams had told me, "Don, you are one of the greatest basketball players ever to come out of New Castle, but one thing you never did — you never made the first team with Jesus Christ!"

Jack's own life reflected the "love, joy and peace" that he always talked about. Those were his fruits, but mine were like spoiled apples and rotten tomatoes — meanness and unhappiness.

I knew there was a real change in Donna since she had "given her heart to Jesus." No more badgering, no more nagging — only an acceptance of things as they were. She must have meant it when she said, "I've given it all to the Lord. It's up to Jesus whether we make it or not."

How I wanted to "make it." I wanted Donna, Donnie, Doug and Don to stay together as a family. "Oh, Lord, what have I done? I don't want this mess!" I cried inside.

On a chilly November day in 1974, I reached for the Bible while I sat in my living room contemplating what was going to become of us. I knew little of what was in it, but I knew I needed something. I came across the scripture in Mark which read, *"For whosoever will save his life shall not lose it, but whosoever shall lose his life for my sake and the gospels— the same shall save it. For what shall it profit a man if he shall gain the whole world, and lose his own soul?"*

"Lose his own soul" — man, was I ever losing — my soul — my family — my very existence!

Stricken with grief by the state of my life, I fell to my knees and prayed, "Lord Jesus, here I am — I've sinned so much that I couldn't even begin to tell you all the rotten things I've done, but I'm sure you know them all. Sometimes I've been too drunk to even remember! I've made a terrible mess of it all, and now I give it all to You!"

Tears of repentance streamed down my cheeks. A beautiful peace swept over me, and I knew I mattered. Right there and then I felt His cleansing, and He accepted me as His son. I was the prodigal who had come home!

Rising from my knees later, I walked to the window and watched my youngest son come up the drive. Doug was eleven then — how much I had missed while raising him! For the first time I welcomed him home with open arms.

Donnie arrived an hour later. I couldn't help but think of the conversation we'd held two days before when I'd come home from the motel and sat in our kitchen. I'd said, "We're losing our motel and five cars. I'm a loser, but I don't know what to do about it."

My namesake's answer had torn my heart, "We know you are, Dad. We love you, but you won't let us help you."

I thought of his words as he entered the door. Reaching out, I welcomed him home, too. I love them both — my two sons — and my Donna. When she arrived home that night, we had a special kind of a "Love-in." Joy and laughter overflowed as they never had before in the Reed household.

Donna and I talked long into the night. Jesus had already begun the healing of our broken marriage and broken hearts.

Over twenty years have passed since that time, and so much has happened. Jesus has opened the door to a ministry for me to many broken men and women. At the beginning I thought I would have to close my accounting office and go into full-time evangelism, but I learned that was what He wanted for me then. The Town House Motel where I'd had my office was repossessed, so I had no choice but to open my place of business in the basement of our home. When I sat across the desk from people who came to have their taxes made out, the Lord gave me an insight into their needs so that I could witness to them.

One of the things that has changed drastically in my life has been the use of my time. I have found I have to spend time every morning in prayer and quiet, seeking the will of the Lord in order to fulfill my need for His direction.

When Donna and I embarked on our new venture in Jesus, we owed 30 financial institutions. Bankruptcy seemed the only way out, but I got a definite "No!" from the Lord. He assured me through prayer that leaving my innocent creditors holding the bag was being a poor witness.

One day while I was in prayer in my office, Jesus visited me and said, "My son, I must do in you in four years what I did in Moses in forty years because time is so short. The last thing they did at the foot of the cross was gamble. Now I commission you to warn the world about gambling and alcohol, but your mission is to the gambler first. Remember, you do not put a needle in your arm to gamble, and it is a hidden cancer that is spreading over the entire world. I detest gambling and no Christian had better attempt to approach My throne with his bags full of bingo and lottery and horse racing stubs. If you give more to gambling or alcohol, then they are idols in your eyes and *I will spew you out of my mouth."* (Rev. 3:16).

I have "Crossed Paths" with thousands of people in the past years, and each day I find myself searching His Word and seeking more and more of His guidance. My office, which my brother-in-law and one of my employees helped build in my cellar, became my sanctuary. Every time I pray, I feel His message to me is urgent, "The Word — the Word — get deeper into My Word!"

During my walk with Him, I have come to see things through His eyes. I see His concept of the corruption in the churches. In a vision I have seen Him standing at the altar of a church. Arms folded, He stood there surveying the gambling, the games, the wild parties which go on within the walls which were built to house His worshippers — not gambling games!

In the vision I saw His eyes — eyes of a wounded Jesus as He surveyed the desecration of His churches. I think of how He bore all the sins of the world on a cross two thousand years ago, and I want to cry out, "Are we going to crucify Him forever by the misuse of His name and His house?"

"That's ridiculous!" people scoff. "The churches aren't that bad!"

Oh, no? I heard about a "Horse Racing Party" held for a retiring minister. Guests placed their bets on horses they watched on a movie screen shown in the church, and then the winnings were given to the honored preacher for a going away gift!

Bingo games are sponsored by churches — carnivals are held in church yards and I see nothing different there than I saw in Vegas. Gambling fever runs rampant as men and women try to win big stakes.

In the book of Mark, Christ stormed the temple and tossed out the money changers who were desecrating His house, but still we continue to use His sacred home for betting and raffling.

Booze, gambling games, carnival atmosphere, wild drinking parties are all put on outside the "House of the Lord" — supposedly to make money for the furthering of His work!

During tax seasons I become painfully aware of where people's hearts and pocketbooks really lie. So called "Born-again Christians" appear at my office with grocery sacks filled with lottery stubs and horse racing receipts that they hope to deduct from their income tax. Surely this grieves the Lord.

I can never thank or praise Him enough for lifting me from my path of destruction I had made for myself. Now I walk with Him to the heights of inner peace and joy.

The pieces of the broken shell that I had become have slowly been put back together. It has not been easy for Donna and me to climb out of our financial hole, nor should it be. We would never have appreciated His constant faithfulness if He had solved our money problems instantaneously. However, the Lord helped us to pay off all our creditors. What a thrill to be able to say to my wife, using her nickname, "Duke, I paid off the last creditor from my gambling debts today. Praise the Lord!"

Donna and I have had to pray and work in His will to find new fulfillment in our marriage. We have had to labor hard to get ourselves back on our feet, but the Lord was faithful because we were faithful to Him.

We still experience setbacks. I would be a liar if I told you that all of our outer circumstances are perfect, for I am certain they never will be. But our walk in faith has made us aware that now we can overcome — but only as we learn to lean on His everlasting arms.

During the more than twenty-years that I have known the Lord, Jesus has helped expand our business. Don, Jr., and I established Reed & Reed Accounting and have moved into elegant offices in Hermitage, PA — a long way from doing our accounting in the basement of our home.

Donna is currently a real estate broker and has her own office building in Hermitage as the owner of Century 21.

Doug married a nurse named Sue. As an engineer he has a great job in Wisconsin. Their first son, Brandon, was joined by identical twin brothers, Tim and Tyler, three and a half years later. On June 24th of this year Benjamin and Daniel, ANOTHER SET OF IDENTICAL TWINS miraculously arrived after many months of bed rest and hardships. The

Lord is good. Doug has his own basketball team.

Don, Jr., and Karen have three growing offspring. Nicki and Shelly are in their teens. Warren, still in elementary school, is a real Reed character!

Years ago God gave me a vision of "Crossing Paths Ministry" expanding from a local Bible Study to a nationwide TV show featuring testimonies of people from all backgrounds who have been plagued with all kinds of problems. We've had Mafia members, former homosexuals and lesbians, men and women from broken homes and broken marriages — the list is seemingly endless. Each testified — first on our radio show— then on local TV. Now the Lord has given us the opportunity to go cross country with our television shows on Sky Angel, letting people personally tell of the dramatic changes in their lives after Crossing Paths with Jesus.

All of this would not have been possible without the help of my co-host, Gene Blakeman, and his dear wife, Pam. When my faith falters in the heat of the bottle that sometimes takes place in the ministry, he is like Aaron and his holding up Moses' arms when Moses became weak. (Exodus 17:12) Ours is a very special relationship. Gene does much of the teaching at our Bible Study; he and Pam and their daughter Theresa all work together setting up banquets which we hold twice a year. Among our featured guests were Tom Papania, one of the former leaders of the New York Mafia, and Jim Irwin, one of the astronauts to walk on the moon.

Ours is a small ministry, but the Lord has let it have a big impact on people's lives. Crossing Paths is currently shown over secular Channel 33 out of Youngstown, OH. The Lord is good!

The Reed Family has no special in-road into Jesus' love that you, too, don't have access to. He's waiting for you to invite Him into your heart so that you might come to enjoy Divine Fellowship with Him. He can carry you through any earthly tribulation!

As a team, you and Jesus can't be beat! Try Him! There's nothing on earth more heavenly than playing on the first team with JESUS!

*****

Don Reed's entire life story is told through "Now I'll Bet on You, Lord!" published by Son-Rise Publications. It is available from Crossing Paths Ministry, P.O. Box 1181, Hermitage, PA 16148 — 724-981-7777. Don can also be reached at that phone number and address. Crossing Path's TV program is available through Sky Angel. Most of the awesome testimonies confined within the covers of this book came about from appearances on Crossing Path's radio or television programs.

Don and Donna Reed

Imprisonment to Empowerment

Carl (Gene) Blakeman & Pam

Tense, I grappled for my handkerchief and gripped the banister at the top of the stairs. Breathing deeply didn't help. I didn't want to be at Republic Steel. I had come upstairs to change my clothes. Now I had to go down among my co-workers.

Fright clutched at me as though it were a living thing. I didn't want to work - not because I was lazy, but because I was terrified of meeting and speaking with people.

To hide my face, I pretended to blow my nose as I descended. Beads of perspiration formed on my forehead. My knees felt weak. My hands, moist from sweat, clung to the banister. At last I was on the bottom step. I hurried to a corner. How could a grown man be so frightened of meeting people? All I knew was that this phobia had a strangle hold on me. Five to fifteen minutes lapsed before I could begin to function properly. Every new day echoed the day before.

I needed help. Where could I find it? At home, I remembered the Bible in the closet, dug it out, and began to read. It was dry and uninteresting. I didn't know that Jesus in a person's heart would make a difference. All I knew was that life was getting so burdensome that I couldn't stand it.

Pam, my wife, looked sympathetically at me. "Gene, I'm going to have the preacher come over."

"Let me know when he's coming, and I won't be here."

Unwittingly turning my back on available help, I groped for other answers. Maybe nerve pills would help.

They didn't.

Because of my phobia, things continued to get worse at work. Each day, life got more intolerable. Standing 150 feet above the blast furnace floor, I glanced down. There was an answer. *One leap and this would be all over.* This thought wormed its way into my mind a number of times. How was I to know that it was Satan, the evil one who stalks around like an angry lion, seeking whom he may devour? Unknown to me, Jesus was protecting me.

Although timidness had shadowed me all my life, it had not always been so overpowering. I had made good grades — 24 A's — when I finished sixth grade. I loved to hunt and fish. During my seventh year I missed a lot of school. My parents didn't make me go. As a result, I made 24 F's and had to repeat the grade. Eighth grade, too, found me hunting and fishing instead of going to school; thus, I failed. The next year I remained out of school, living with my grandmother and worked for my uncle in a sawmill. I reached the six-foot mark and longed to play basketball, so I returned to school. I had to repeat the eighth grade. That would have been bad enough, but the coach and I couldn't get along. I quit school. This gave me a tremendous inferiority complex.

At sixteen, I got a job with the A & P Tea Company in Youngstown, Ohio. After a year I went to a machine shop. At eighteen, I got a job with Republic Steel in Youngstown.

You would think, as time progressed, that someone would have recognized my misery and steered me toward help, but apparently, I was able to camouflage my problem very well. I was offered a foreman's job. I turned it down. I never told them why. I knew I'd have to meet people and talk with strangers. I couldn't handle that.

All my life I'd been timid, but shyness became a dragon that breathed down the back of my neck. It chased me through life; time only made the monster grow more victims.

I began social drinking; using alcohol as a crutch seemed to make it easier for me to carry on a conversation. Then I went out almost every night and got about half drunk. Drinking wasn't the answer, but I didn't know what was. I was searching, but in the wrong places.

Easter 1966 was approaching.

"Dad, you're going with us Easter Sunday to see us in the church program, aren't you?"

"Well..." I grappled for an excuse because the thought of mingling with unfamiliar people terrified me. "If I have off work," I said, figuring that I'd probably have to work and the excuse sounded legitimate.

The closer the date grew, the more scared I felt. God knew things I didn't. He managed to have that Easter Sunday an off-work day for me. I searched for another excuse.

"Pam, I don't have clothes to wear to church."

"We'll get you a suit."

This we did. We planned to get up early, so we would have lots of time. That might have helped, but everything went wrong.

We had five kids at that time. They and Pam piled into the car. Fear twisted my stomach. Cold beads of moisture dappled my forehead before I got behind the wheel. A couple of miles down the road I was beginning to panic. My fingers gripped the wheel. The closer to the church we got, the more scared I became. I swallowed hard. "We're going to be late, and I'm not going in," I said.

Pam looked at her watch. "We have five minutes."

At the church, my terror overwhelmed me. There were a lot of parked cars, and people were waiting inside to greet me. My heart was tapping a staccato rhythm against my ribs; I felt sick. "We're late. I'm not going in."

The kids were excited about being in the program. I was fighting them, but I was so scared I couldn't help it.

"I'll just drop you off."

"No, Dad! You have to come in and see us perform."

"I said, I'll drive up to the ramp and let you off."

"Please come in with us, Dad."

Guilt and shyness were playing tag in my stomach, and fright frolicked with them both. My family's pleas were making me mad. I gritted my teeth as I pulled to a stop. "Get out!"

Tears ran down Pam's face. My kids were all crying. I felt terrible, but I couldn't help it. The monster the fear had become was not only devouring my life, it was destroying my relationship with my family.

I watched them go into the church and started to cry. *I should park and go in.* **Fear** clawed at my insides and won the battle; however, before I pulled out of the driveway, I was really suffering over how I'd disappointed Pam and the kids. Unknown to me, this was the workings of the true God. I felt drawn to church. But people were waiting in there to meet me! *There are other churches. I'll stop at one of them.*

Intentions were good. Actions failed. I did not recognize the moving of the Holy Spirit, but He was at work in me.

At home, I hurried to the television, snapped it on, and searched for a church service. As I listened to the preacher, I began to cry. God began to soften my heart. At thirty-one, I was finally coming to the Lord. We had a hardwood floor in the room. I knelt, tears streaming down my face. I was ready to accept Jesus into my heart, but I needed guidance. The program came to a close. It was too abrupt. I knew I needed God. I searched for another program but couldn't find one. I wept until there was a puddle of tears on the wooden floor. Sin, of which I was now aware, burdened me. I realized what I had been doing to my family, and I knew I had to ask them to forgive me. Where could I look for help?

The Bible. I retrieved it, sat in a big chair, and began to read. I remembered hearing a preacher once say, "The Bible keeps us from sin, or sin keeps us from the Bible." He was right. I was amazed at how alive the Word now seemed; still, I needed more. I promised God, "I'll go to church from now on."

My family returned from church. I met them in the middle

of the living room, tears running down my face. "I was wrong. I know I hurt you. Will you forgive me?"

They all did.

"What goes on at church on Sunday night?"

Pam hadn't been going, but she knew what happened. "The preacher talks about Jesus."

"We're going."

Since I had shunned the people who were waiting at the church door to meet me in the morning, it was more difficult to go in the evening. Still, I kept my promise to God. He gave me strength and courage. God was beginning to work a miracle in me!

I was under conviction, but I didn't get saved the first night. The church was having revival meetings the next week. My parents had been Christians, but they had slipped away from the Lord. Monday night, my mother went to church, too. During the altar call, my heart started to pound. I thought it was because I was tired. The workings of the Lord were new to me. My ten-year-old son went forward. After the service, I asked him what had happened.

"Oh, Dad," he said, "it's so nice to have Jesus come and sit down beside you."

The next night, during the altar call, Mom took my hand and we went forward. She found her way back to the Lord that night. Later Dad did too.

I was on my knees, crying. The presence of God came over me. It was like an electric feeling. There were pins and needles all over me, yet I wondered where the peace was that I was supposed to experience.

My brother-in-law rested a hand on my shoulder. "It's a matter of faith, Gene. You have to believe."

Romans 10:9-10. *"If thou shalt confess with thy mouth the Lord Jesus, and shalt believe in thine heart that God has raised him from the dead, thou shalt be saved."*

The revelation struck me. My tears vanished, and I felt a glowing happiness that I'd never known. Looking back, I thanked God for His grace and mercy in protecting me when

I could have easily taken my life.

Later I discovered that Pam and the kids had all come forward and been saved, too. Crossing paths with Jesus made a fantastic difference in our lives. We were never the same after meeting the Son of God. Pam had gone to church for six years and hadn't known she wasn't saved.

"Except a man be born of water and of the Spirit, he cannot enter into the Kingdom of God...Ye must be born again."
John 3:5,7

Since 1975 I've been in the ministry. After I became saved, I received power. My fear diminished. I became more brave for Jesus. I could preach and teach. Meeting people was no longer the fright it had been. After Jesus came into my heart, the Bible came alive. Later I found the power of the baptism of the Holy Ghost with the evidence of speaking in tongues. That was when God called me into the ministry. Had I not had that experience, I would not be in the preaching ministry today.

I found a rest. I found a peace. I found a strength. I found a boldness that I'd never had in my life before. I also got my high school diploma.

I went from ready to leap to my death from 150 feet above the blast furnace to witnessing about Christ — not only to individuals, but I had a radio program and became the co-host of *Crossing Paths*, a Christian television talk show. Jesus is real and alive. I came from being imprisoned by fear to being empowered by the Holy Spirit. Through experience, Matthew 11:28-30 became precious to me.

"Come unto me, all ye who labor and are heavy laden, and I will give you rest. Take my yoke upon you, and learn of me; for I am meek and lowly in heart: and ye shall find rest unto your souls. For my yoke is easy, and my burden is light."

When we accept Christ, He cleanses us from sin and writes our names in the Lamb's Book of Life. He empowers us with the Holy Spirit. He gives rest. He gives peace. He gives strength. He gives boldness.

He sets the prisoners free!

* * * * *

Why not invite Jesus into your heart today? He will change your life forever!

You can contact Gene at:
Crossing Paths Ministry
PO Box 1181
Hermitage, PA 16148
(724) 981-7777
or write to him at:
Blakeman Ministries
PO Box 364
North Lima, OH 44452

Mission Impossible

Testimony of Ann Joyce Titus (with Russian "grandma")

A quick rap on my bedroom door tells me it is Sunday, and Daddy is expecting my sister Jean and me to be ready on time. I am just old enough to remember that there was an era when children did not argue with their fathers...thus I grew up attending church each and every Sunday.

In my teens during a Communion Service at the Central Christian Church, the Lord got my attention. As a visitor this particular Sunday, and even though I do not remember the exact words, the pastor spoke during the invitation, he reminded the congregation the only requirement to participate was that, "You have already invited Jesus to be your Saviour."

Not sure that I'd really ever done that, quietly I said, "Jesus, I believe you died for me...I want You in my heart...Please!" Nothing dramatic...no big change in my life...only I knew the difference inside!

Time marched on. After graduation from Sharon High School in 1952, I started my first real job at the large Westinghouse Plant. I joined in with a group of young people who went to a popular dance hall called "Shady Grove," where they had round, square, and polka dancing every

Thursday night. The second time there, a tall, smiling, redhead asked me to join him for a set of square dances. Six months later Wayne Titus and I were married at the Clark Methodist Church, Clark, PA. My heart was pounding as I stood at the altar pledging to "love, honor, and cherish...till death do us part."

Ours was a wonderful marriage. They say opposites attract, and, indeed, we were opposite. Wayne was quiet, patient, gentle, and loving. I was loving, not real quiet or very patient. Basically, I acted on impulse. During the next few years Sherry, Jeff, and Pam joined the household. Because Wayne and I loved Jesus, we wanted our children to know Him...so just as our parents before us...church was a regular part of our life.

We'd been married only ten years, when Wayne developed heart problems. After many tests, including a heart catherization, we were told my husband had to have open heart surgery. Up to this point of my life, I had always felt there was SOMEONE to help — my parents, my friends, yes, even Blue Cross/Blue Shield. The night before Wayne's operation, I never felt so alone, so abandoned, so scared! Who could help now? Had I ever really learned to trust Jesus?

The next 14 years were "Good News...Bad News" years. Wayne was in and out of several hospitals...open heart surgery twice...later a total hip replacement.

I watched my husband during this time — watched him in his quiet way witness to everyone around him...be it family, nurses, doctors, or other patients. His light was always shining. I was told after Wayne's first operation he could expect a good five more years, but he lived an additional 13...and on October 19, 1980, the Lord took him home.

By this time I had taken a job at the Welfare Office in Hermitage, PA. I was also involved in my local church, Women's Aglow Fellowship, the "Jesus" events at the Watson Farm in Mercer, PA...as well as being producer for a local TV show called "Crossing Paths." Keeping busy helped keep me from missing my husband; therefore, I never thought of this time as BASIC TRAINING...HOWEVER...

In 1993 Rev. Jack Stevenson invited me to go to Russia as a short-term missionary. "Jack," I answered, "I can't do that," then listed my many reasons why not.

Rev. Jack was on the first team to get into Khabarovsk, Russia, Far East, where he spent the entire year of 1994. When he returned, all we heard was "RUSSIA — RUSSIA — RUSSIA!"

Early in 1996 Jack again asked, "Have you changed your mind about Russia?" He told me that a new team was going in January 1997, and would I please pray about my involvement.

I thought to myself..."Surely, it could not hurt to pray about it"...so pray I did. With a long list of reasons why I could not possibly go, I approached the Lord daily. A big reason I felt I could not leave the U.S. was I had developed a Poly Neuropathy and was having a lot of problems walking. My family physician had already started me on B12 shots, and he felt I would surely improve. One by one, all of the other problems I faced were answered — right down to a young man offering to rent my home while I was away.

The last hurdle to cross was raising $23,000 support. EASY!! I would just ask 23 people to pledge $1,000 each. NOT SO EASY!! A few people did give me $1,000...the rest of the pledges came $10 — $15 — $20 a month. I soon had received the total amount I needed and found that I now had many, many, many more than 23 friends praying for and supporting me in Russia...(It was not until months later when all the cards and letters arrived in Khabarovsk did I realize this.)

It would take volumes to share my feelings as I waited one week in Anchorage, Alaska, for our plane to take off. There was Charlene Reitz, my roommate — a true sister in Christ; T.J. Horne — our team leader; Sue Fuller — who was returning to complete her third year; Rev. Jack — team shepherd, and me. We were told it was 30° below zero with high winds and not safe to land. Day after day, sitting there in the airport, I would ask, "Lord, are you sure this is where I am supposed to be?"

Finally the wind calmed down and off we flew, arriving in Khabarovsk on February 2, 1997.

YES! It was cold! I moved quickly out of the airport toward a group of smiling faces. During the months to follow, I discovered it is an honored thing to greet people at the airport. Standing there in the frigid air was the rest of our team — Russian Nationals, who would soon become an important part of my team life and our drivers for the trip. Everyone began throwing suitcases into auto trunks and two small vans. Quickly we were seated and driven to our fifth-floor flat.

I have no idea how all of my belongings arrived safely, but there were my suitcases...stored just inside the front door. Charlene and I breathed a quick prayer for those responsible...and began to explore our new home. We were in a very small, very neat two-bedroom flat with a tiny kitchen and even smaller bath. But truly we had everything we needed, including a Russian electric iron and ironing board. We were blessed!

The next few days Jack, T.J., Charlene, and I explored the city. Khabarovsk was much larger and more beautiful than I expected. Even more exciting than finding such a city was the beauty of the men and women we were meeting.

During our orientation we were told, "Expect to receive much more than you can ever hope to give." I was beginning to see how true this was. One of our first new friends was a woman named Helen. She lived just below us on the third floor, and we were told she spoke English. One morning on the way out the door, Charlene and I decided to stop and introduce ourselves. I now believe this was the beginning of our miracle...

"Come in, Come in," she invited...and our relationship began. During the months to follow, we shared our lives. Helen, like so many in Russia, had a mother who believed in Jesus; but during the 80 years of Communist reign, they were not free to worship as they pleased. We shared everything from recipes to raising children. Helen was delighted to take us shopping and introduced us to the tellers in the local bank. She explained to everyone, "They are Americans, and you must help them." Helen and her husband took us into their home, into their hearts.

Within two weeks I met a young pastor named Uhri, a man from whom you could feel the Spirit emulating. He spoke no English. I knew ten words in Russian...we instantly became friends. Uhri had been praying for someone to help him start a home Bible study group. Within a month we had a Monday and a Thursday evening group started.

Watching the Lord move in these meetings made Charlene and me realize how blessed we were to have been invited to be a part of God's work in this country. How exciting to know we were a tiny part of His Will for this part of the world.

Months later an American friend came to Khabarovsk to visit, and I took Ron to our Monday Bible Study. Within minutes he leaned over and asked if it was always like this.

"What do you mean?" I asked.

"I mean the presence of the Holy Spirit," was his answer.

Indeed, the Holy Spirit was the leader of this group. It was simply our privilege to be there with Him.

You must understand that all of this was done through a translator. Andrey became my voice, my Russian Guardian Angel, and my cane. Yes, I was still having trouble walking...and knowing we were on at least 10 inches of ice...his young, strong arm was indeed a comfort.

What I appreciated most about Andrey was his ability to translate not only my words, but also my feelings. He generally caught a jist and could transmit this to whatever audience we were speaking to.

Invitations came quickly now...we began sharing the Jesus film (the story of the life of Christ in the book of Luke.) I was not prepared for the response. This is a four-hour movie. We would show two hours of the movie the first week and the second two hours the following week. Young and old alike sat and watched without moving a muscle. Tears would flow from the faces of old ladies as they repeated the prayer at the end of the film.

Our team learned of an old men's home in the city which housed not only older men but also older women, and disabled persons as well. Wednesday was to be team day. However, we found we could squeeze in all the business of the day, have team devotions, lunch, and then move on to the home in time to have a short program and visit with the residents. Usually we spent a few hours moving from tiny room to tiny room (again through a translator), simply saying hello...letting people know we cared. Months later when five new members joined our team, the new team came with guitars and the enthusiasm of a new generation. Our visit days later turned into a loving Bible Study. The director of the home told us quite frankly, "I am an ex-communist. Your beliefs are not mine, but as long as you do not hurt my people, you are welcome to come in each week." WE PROMISED NOT TO HURT ANYONE.

With all we had to do, my greatest joy was in the one-on-one contacts we had. It was through the personal contacts that Jesus taught me the greatest lessons. One freezing cold morning in March, I was to have gone to school with Tom (another team member). I was dumbfounded when my driver simply forgot to pick me up. For a few seconds anger started to swell up, so I said a quick prayer..." OK, Lord...I guess you have something else in mind for today." With difficulty, I climbed the five flights of stairs back to my flat. I found Charlene reading from Proverbs. I joined her in Chapter 18 verse 24, *"A man of many friends comes to ruin, but there is a friend who sticks closer than a brother."*

As we were reading, Irene came to our door. We invited her in. She hesitated, not wanting to bother us. We insisted she stay and join in. Charlene re-read the Scripture, and Charlene asked Irene what she thought it meant.

"Very easy," came her reply, and she went on to describe her life. "When I was living in Moscow and going to school, I lived with a young man who had lots of money, and many friends. We had an exciting life together. All too soon, he had to return to his home in France. I was left with no money, no school and no friends. I was also on the verge of a nervous breakdown."

"But who is this friend who sticks closer than a brother?" we asked. Within a short time Irene prayed and invited our Best Friend into her heart. Jesus certainly did have a plan for us that day!

I am often asked, "What was the hardest thing you had to do in Russia?"

My answer..."LEAVE!" Leave all the dear friends — my translators, the doctors we worked with in the Doctors College, and the young Russian students who often visited our flat. We lived just across the street from a large university, and many of the students would drop in for a Coke and my homemade cookies.

There was Natasha, my language coach, who was young enough to be my daughter. I admit that I did not learn a lot of the language, but I did learn to love Natasha.

Leave Natalie, my Russian Granddaughter? Lord, I would think...it's not fair. I wept as I began preparing for my trip back home. When will I ever see my friends?

Again, the hand of Jesus. Natalie has completed Khabarovsk Teachers University, majoring in English and French, and was accepted to study at Taylor University in Upland, Indiana, starting in September of 1998. Upland is only six hours from my home so she will be able to spend vacations with my family. Another blessing!

I praise the Lord that I was a tiny part of His plan for the Russian people. "WHAT NEXT?" Do I have any plans to return to Russia? My only thought now is to dedicate 1997 to Him as a training program and continue to seek Him...day by day. The Lord says that we're to feed the hungry and take care of His little ones. That's in my heart cry.

I WILL WAIT FOR WHAT HE WANTS ME TO DO NEXT.

In the meantime I see part of my love for Jesus in Natalie, who bubbles with enthusiasm whether she is signing for the deaf, ministering in churches, reaching out to the elderly, or teaching the children. She never seems to run out of enthusiasm. The joy that causes her face to shine makes others want to know her secret. Her answer? "The love of Jesus!" Such a thrill to have her here in the States where I can still see her in person!

My other dear friends back in Russia are constantly in my prayers, for I have seen and experienced first-hand their economic hardships which seem to worsen each day. Email letters from the other missionaries still there tell of the hospitals not having enough food to feed their patients. Orphanages have so little help and resources that the babies are left in their cribs without diapers. The last report from them said that those tiny infants are only getting three small feedings a day. When I came home, I helped found the Jabez Foundation to help the Russian people and especially those tiny, forgotten orphans that no one can care for properly.

* * * * *

Joyce Titus can be reached for speaking engagements or information about Russia at 675 Clay Furnace Rd., Sharpsville, PA 16150.

Natalie Sizikova and Joyce Titus

Missionary Star

Natalie Sizikova

Four years ago I met five American missionaries who came to Khabarovsk, a remote city in far eastern Russia, located about thirty miles from the China border. Led by the missionary star, and following God's command to "go and preach the Good News," they crossed the North Pacific Ocean in order to share the gospel with high school and college students in that "forgotten by God and people" place. The encounter with these "brave American trespassers," who not so long ago were considered to be the worst enemies of Communism, radically changed my life forever. Struggling with a confusing culture, the invincible Russian language, and skeptical hostility towards any kind of foreign missionaries, they managed to teach me how to play American sports, cook pizzas, and use their lap-top computers, and even more importantly, how to read and understand the Bible, love unconditionally, give willingly, have joy and live freely.

In order for you to see what this encounter meant to me, I should start with my background. I grew up in the very conservative Russian Orthodox church. My grandmother used to teach me about the Trinity and the Virgin Mary and read about the holy lives of the ancient saints. Since my childhood she used to take me to the Sunday sunrise services, called Divine Liturgy, where I would sing in the choir with a few other grannies. Always ashamed to admit that I wasn't able to understand the lyrics of the Old Russian hymns dating back to 15-16 centuries, I just followed the monotonous music. Being a sixteen-year-old high school girl charmed by fashion magazines, popular movies, and "wild" peers, I was the youngest among the "respectful age" choir singers. Immediately I became a sure target for their strict instructions:"Braid your hair, cover your head properly with a kerchief, and don't walk in front of the altar! Put the candles for the living on the right side, and for the dead on the left! Remember to bow to the priest when he passes by." They would critically examine the length of my skirt (knee length was too short, to say nothing about mini), and disapprovingly comment on the amount of my jewelry and make-up (having none was the best).

Being trapped in all these religious rules and traditions, I saw no escape from its overloading burden. Lonely and miserable, I felt like an awkward elephant in the fragile glass palace, afraid to move or breathe, scared to live. I used to think of Heaven as the highest court where we all would be judged someday. I did not know how to pray, so I'd repeat, "Our Heavenly Father," the only prayer Grandma taught me. I remember lifting up my eyes towards the lavishly decorated golden cupola (dome) depicting God, the Ruler of the Universe. I thought that He was sitting up there with all the saints to judge and punish such "unholy" people as me. I felt as if I were the worst criminal on Earth - no hope to be forgiven, sentenced to die.

It wasn't until I became a freshman at the Teacher's Training University that I met the first Americans in my life. They were God's messengers - missionaries (three men and two women) who brought the ray of Light and New Hope to me, and whose faithful witness greatly influenced my whole life. They came with legal permission from the local officials to organize a Christian Student Center for the youth and to work as English teachers at my university.

Looking back at the past, I am still amazed at how quickly

I became friends with them and learned how to trust them in spite of all the "cold war" lies I was told. Soon, I realized that these Americans were not so "bad," after all. In fact, their doors were always open for their curious Russian visitors. They were ready to talk and ready to listen. I remember spending two or three hours on the phone with Connie Robins, my English teacher, who would patiently answer all my "silly" questions about the American people, culture, and its political system. One day she invited me to her house and we listened to what she called "contemporary Christian music" — Amy Grant, Twila Paris, and Michael Card. I really enjoyed it because I could UNDERSTAND what the songs were about but was greatly surprised that it was permissible to praise and worship God NOT only in church, but also in EVERYDAY life.

Some time later, Connie invited me to come to their Bible study at the Christian Student Center in order to practice my English and at the same time to discuss some issues from the Bible. Well, I NEVER was able to comprehend this Divine book to start with. Just like any Russian Orthodox, I kept a copy of it at home with the only application being to wipe the dust off its cover. Its content seemed to be so complicated and boring, and its Old Russian language was at the same time so hard for me to decipher, as if it were written in Chinese characters. At the same time I knew that the Bible was a Holy book, to be read by the highest priest solely in church.

Can you imagine my reaction when I saw that these American missionaries not only could read and UNDERSTAND the Bible, but they freely QUOTED it and DISCUSSED it without a "special benediction" of the priest. In fact, they were not even dressed properly for such solemn procedure. Connie wore plain blue jeans and a sweat shirt, not a sign of a kerchief or a modest long skirt. Others had an even "more disrespectful" look — shorts, T-shirts and baseball caps. It wasn't their "out of place" outfits or "fanatically" passionate way to praise and pray to God that impressed me the most, but the stream of unknown, bold, and, at the same time, very gentle, "out of place" LOVE. Unselfish and pure, it radiated from their eyes and motivated all their actions. I could neither explain nor comprehend it; I just needed it very badly.

I could not understand why these people, who obviously had a much better life in America, gave up everything they had, including modern conveniences, families and careers, in order to come to such a shocking (for any Western mind) hard-to-survive, place. Their daily life was just like a "normal" daily life for any Russian, full of unpredictable surprises. No gas for three weeks, no electricity at night, no central heating or hot water during the winter time became their choice! I thought they might be crazy to trade their nothing-to-worry-about, luxurious American life for such miserable survival. In fact, they were even happy and never complained whatsoever.

They shared with us the secrets of American pizza and chocolate chip cookies. We introduced them to Russian traditional borsh and pelemeni. We had lots of fun learning how to play American football and after each game I would try to find out more about "their God" and His unknown love. I began to attend the Bible studies regularly, improving both my English and my attitude toward the Bible.

A month later I went to the first Christian winter camp. There I accepted Jesus Christ as my personal Savior. For the first time in my life I prayed with my OWN words, simply asking Jesus not only to be a severe Judge, but a kind and loving Friend to me. For the first time ever I felt free and forgiven; for the first time I cried with the tears of overwhelming joy, and not of sorrow.

Finally it dawned on me that God sent His messengers to deliver me from a prison of fear and religious misconceptions. It was the same Redeeming love which set me free, that guided their way across the borders and oceans as they faithfully carried the good news to all "the weary and lost." This unconditional LOVE was shining brightly like a navigating star in the dark night skies, calling me to join His mission too, and witness to my relatives, friends, and a great big world which is desperately searching for peace and a new hope.

The Lord has blessed me abundantly since I came to know Him. My beloved Mother also accepted Jesus as her personal Lord and Savior while viewing the film showing The Master's name.

My father and mother reluctantly agreed to let their only child come to America to attend school. I know what a sacrifice that decision was for them. The heart-cry of my homeland — their need of the Savior and the desperation of their physical lives — has prompted me to attend Taylor University in Upland, Indiana. America and Americans have graciously opened their hearts, their homes and their pocketbooks to me so that I might get a degree in business administration and the go home to Russia where I will share what I learned from Christians that there is a Blessed Hope for them as well as the rest of the world.

That Hope is Jesus Christ.

* * * * *

Natalie Sizikova is currently attending Taylor University and can be reached at P.O. Box 556, Upland, Indiana 46989.

They Called Me "Hansi"

Maria Anne Hirschmann's story

The slim figure of the white-haired peasant woman vanished into a hazy distance as the little train engine puffed itself into more smoke and speed.

In my ears rang the last words my foster mother had said as I boarded the country train which would take me to Prague, the capital of my homeland Czechoslovakia.

"Marichen, Vergiss Jesus Nicht," she had admonished, and I nodded and waved through smiles and tears. I left excited and scared, happy and sad; and her words left me confused.

Why should I forget Jesus, I wondered. I had heard about Him and prayed to God as long as I could remember. My foster mother had taken me in for Christ's and pity's sake, in spite of abject poverty and her husband's anger because food was scarce even for their own four children. Mother often had to share her own meager portions with me, and both of us stayed very slim. I slept in a hayloft and loved to pray when the darkness closed in on me, but I wasn't sure if God listened. I was always naughty and God rewarded good behavior only! He probably did not even know my name since I was an orphan and the poorest kid of the village.

The next two years my life had changed dramatically. The whirlwind began when Adolph Hitler's troops marched into the German territories of our country. Later he also annexed the rest of the land, and all of Czechoslovakia was now protected by the Third Reich of Nazi Germany. Everybody was scared at first, but Hitler had kept his promise: Sudeten-land - and had by now food, hope and work for everyone and things looked up. Nazi educators came into our little village school and tested all of us. I received a special scholarship for a leadership training school in Prague in order to become a Nazi youth leader. It was such an honor to be chosen; everybody in the village was proud of me. My foster mother did not seem to share the sentiment. Now I know why! Of course, she was concerned for nothing; I knew all about Jesus, the God of my mother.

It took one short year of Nazi training, and I changed gods. I worshiped Hitler. I believed sincerely that I belonged to the super race, and it was our destiny to conquer the world. Since Word War II was already giving us victory after victory, I had no doubt that the Great Supreme Power had chosen all of us to bring a better way of life to every nation on earth. The war years brought me hardship, sacrifices, higher rank, responsibility, and a sweet romance by mail, with a Navy man.

I never doubted Germany's victory, and the crushing defeat of Nazi Germany caught me totally unprepared and devastated my soul and body.

I ended up in a Communist labor camp in Bohemia and observed the cruelty of race hate in its most brutal form.

Russian soldiers raped and plundered; the Czech overseer used fist and whip freely to get the last bit of work out of us Germans. I finally escaped from my slave masters and went into hiding. In order to get away from harsher punishment, I knew I had to leave my homeland and make my way to West Germany. Someone whispered that I should try for the American Military Zone; it was the safest place to be - and there was even some food available for the incoming refugees from the East!

I didn't believe it! I did not believe anything or anyone anymore! I had turned into an empty young woman — 19 years of age but feeling like 90 years old. I felt numb, betrayed and deeply confused. My ulcered stomach screamed for food. As my girlfriend and I walked for long weeks in the rain, the only edible stuff we could find were herbs, roots, and mushrooms. We forgot how food tasted; we wondered if there was a human being left anywhere who would be willing to give us a helping hand.

Help came. But from the least expected place — from men I feared and despised.

I was still a Nazi, though Nazi Germany had vanished; and I hated those who had destroyed it. I expected any Allied Soldier to act like the Russian Soldiers I had encountered.

I had seen them rape my girlfriend and shoot people at the slightest provocation. When I came face to face with the first American Soldier, I got ready to fight him off and be eventually killed.

To my amazement, American Soldiers gave us our first real meal and drink and offered us a cot to rest. They smiled a lot; they spoke English, which I did not understand, and they never hurt or molested us! Will those unknown GI Soldiers ever know what they did for me? - May God bless them!

It turned my life around, and I knew that someday I would go to America and find out what makes the American people so different!

Yes, I did go to America with my Navy man, whom I married in West Germany, and my two children. After a long wait, we emigrated to the USA in 1955.

I also found out what makes Americans different: America has a Christian heritage and believes in freedom.

I have never found another people who are as willing to help as Americans are!

In West Germany my husband and I had converted to

Christianity after we had gotten married and tried to rebuild our shattered lives. However, we never knew how to apply our new-found faith into our daily lives and struggles until we came to the USA.

Our Christian neighbors taught us more by their willingness to help than by the teaching of doctrine. I couldn't catch what they said until I learned to understand, speak, and read English, but actions always speak louder than words.

One of the hardest things for me to understand was America's way of freedom. I had grown up under total dictatorship from babyhood on. My foster father was a religious legalist who ruled his home with an iron fist. Nazi school reinforced what I already knew: You obey without questioning and follow your leader into death. You wait for orders, you never make your own decisions, you don't have a choice, you are one link in a nation's chain. The individual does not matter ever, "das Volk" (the nation as a whole) is the only thing that matters!

When I came to America, I found a way of life that scared me for the first few years. I didn't have a dictator to tell me what to think or do; the police did not watch when people moved from place to place; and the editorials in the newspaper criticized the American government - and nobody went to jail for it?

How could a country have law and order with such a relaxed attitude? What an unusual way of daily life my neighbors lived - and it all had something to do with "freedom" and "democracy." I did not know what it all meant; so I asked my church friends about it, but nobody could explain it. The first thing about freedom I found out was that Americans have it, use it, take it for granted, and cannot explain it. So I asked the Lord to help me understand it. After all, the Bible told me that Jesus had come to set me free; and I didn't know what that meant, either!

The Lord showed me a statement by William Penn which said that American people had a choice: They could either be governed by God or ruled by tyrants.

The key word for me was "choice!" I did not know that individuals were permitted to have a choice, which demands you have two or more sides to anything.

The brainwashing of my youth always presented only one side; there was never a choice. For the first time in my life I began to understand God's gift to me! HE gives every human being a choice to accept our Heavenly Father's provision for the human race; which is His only son Jesus Christ as our Redeemer, Saviour and Lord. We also may reject HIM - and many people do! God is Love and Love never forces. God's love always gives freedom of choice!

What a gift and what a price Heaven paid to make it available to every human being! Jesus died to give us a choice between heaven and hell.

I fell in love with Jesus. I fell in love with freedom and America, and I understood that to live in a free country is a gift of God. It is also a great responsibility. Free people not only have a choice, they need to make the right choices to stay free. It takes the inner control of the Judeo-Christian ethic with its two sides to choose the good, or freedom becomes a mockery.

It took me a few years to grasp it all; but now I consider my freedom of choice as God's most precious gift, and I handle it with much prayer.

By my choice I became a Christian and was born into the family of God. God never forced me! By my free choice I became a citizen of the USA — nobody forced me to do so! I joined my church because I was free to do so, not because I had to - what a wonderful way to live!

As the years here in America mounted, I experienced also the pain of heavy choices I had to make; and that other people's decisions influence my life deeply.

As my five children grew up, (three more were born in the USA) I had to learn "to let go and let God" guide them because they need to live by their own choices! It hurts a lot more when your mate leaves and remarries. Many Christians blame you for the broken home.

But through all the ups and downs of my turbulent life, Jesus was right beside me - even when I did not believe in HIM anymore. Today I know that someone can be dead sincere - and dead wrong! I was both, but Jesus never removed HIS protection.

Freedom of choice plays a primary role in spiritual growth of a Christian. As we mature in Christ, we often have to make a clear choice to trust and obey Jesus when physical circumstances look forbidding and impossible.

When the Lord nudged me to write my autobiography, I was petrified. I knew my limited ability to express myself in the English language - and my mother tongue was German.

I chose to obey and I learned a big lesson. Jesus loves to do for me what I cannot do by myself. My book became a best-seller and was translated into many languages)*see foot note). My Lord delights to do the impossible.

We forget so easily when things look scary! It became a much harder choice when Jesus encouraged me to leave, after my divorce, a secure position as a master teacher. (I had five children in private schools.)

After much soul searching, I chose to trust Jesus as my provider and began a faith ministry called HANSI. (The Nazi's had given me that name because I was such a tomboy. It means "little Johnny" in German) People had started to call me HANSI after my book became popular and I didn't like it. It brought back painful memories. The Lord comforted me. HE showed me that HE picked that name. It stood for "**H**elp **A**merica to **N**ew **S**piritual **I**nsight."

From that moment, on I felt delighted to be HANSI.

For more than 25 years I had the privilege to serve God and America through my small organization.

Jesus never faileth! HE always provided and HE sent me the help I needed, mainly for travel and speaking appointments. Betty Pershing gave up her financially stable job and her retirement pay to join our "nonprofit" ministry which offered no earthly securities - but we have the promises of God!

I told Betty she didn't need a retirement fund. We'll die with our boots on. To this day, we have not retired, but we still do what we like to do best. Lift up the Name of Jesus so that HE may draw the people close to HIMSELF.

Hansi has become "Grandma Hansi" by now, especially, since I obeyed the Lord and started an orphanage in former Russia, now Belarus - but that is a story of the future — for Jesus still has to do the impossible, the building is only half finished.

Can HE do it? Yes, HE can!

Can I stick with it? Yes, I can do all things through Christ who strengthens me.

And when my Lord calls me home, I leave my boots behind. Jesus has someone who will fit into it to carry on HIS work, I am sure! Better yet, maybe HE will return in my lifetime, and we all shall meet HIM in the air. What a glorious day that will be! Come soon, Lord Jesus!

* * * *

The book *Hansi the Girl Who Left the Swastika* can be ordered from Hansi Ministries, P.O. Box 961, Grand Haven, Michigan 49417. Fax or call (616) 777-0160.

Eternity Assurance

Daniel N. Nasr

"If you are hit by a car and killed when you leave this building, where will you spend eternity?"

I stood on the sidewalk and stared into a busy Cairo street. Thinking about the evangelist's question made me too terrified to cross. My bus stop was on the other side. I had to get home! *But what if I get hit by a car?* The evangelist's words continued to echo through my tormented brain. *Where will you spend eternity? Eternity? Eternity?* Would I go to heaven? *If what the man said about being "born again" is true, I'll go to hell!*

Some may call my terror paranoia, but my fright was real! I had to get home, yet I could not cross the street. I waited for a bus on my side, boarded, and rode to the terminal; then I rode back past my regular stop to get home. I was so thankful to get there safely; however, I didn't feel safe. I went to bed, but I couldn't sleep. Still, the question, "Where will you spend eternity?" haunted me.

The revival I had attended had been an nondenominational evangelistic service. The evangelist talked about the rich man and Lazarus and that there was heaven to gain and hell to shun. I was a religious guy. I was eighteen years old, but I had never heard the meaning of salvation or the term "born again." When he told us there was hell to shun it was new to me.

I tossed and turned. I didn't know that the Holy Spirit was convicting me. *Born again, born again,* ricochetted through my tormented thought and throbbed in my heart.

In John 3:3 and 5 Jesus said, *"I tell you the truth, no one can SEE the kingdom of God unless he is born again...I tell you the truth, no one can ENTER the kingdom of God unless he is born of water and the Spirit."*

In verse 7 Jesus said, *"You should not be surprised at my saying, 'You MUST be born again...'"*

I didn't fully understand. I said, "Jesus, I heard that Scripture and I'm not sure; but if you keep me safe until tomorrow, I'll be the first one forward at the altar call."

The service was at seven o'clock. I was there at six. I prayed, "Jesus, give me the peace that passes all understanding. Give me the assurance that I am saved, born again and ready. I want to know that if I die tonight, I will go to heaven."

I gave my life to Jesus and found the peace I sought. My fear evaporated and my heart rejoiced.

In John 14:26-27 (NIV) Jesus said, *"But the Counselor, the Holy Spirit, whom the Father will send in my name, will teach you all things and will remind you of everything I have said to you. Peace I leave with you: my peace I give you. I do not give to you as the world gives. Do not let your hearts be troubled and do not be afraid."*

I was raised in the Coptic Orthodox Church in Egypt. In my religious teaching, I had never heard of being born again. The terminology was all different, but it's in the Bible! I want every Christian and every friend of mine to read John 3:3, 5 and 7. I want all my Egyptian friends and family to be born again and accept Christ as their personal Savior and Lord as I have.

Christians in Egypt are in the minority and represent 15 percent of the population of about 60 million. The Coptic Orthodox church is about 75 percent of the entire Christian faith; 25 percent are evangelicals and Catholics.

Coptic Orthodox are the real descendants of the pharaohs. They were never mixed with the Arabs as they are historically considered the genuine stock, descendants of the pharaohs. Coptic Orthodox became Christians when St. Mark evangelized Egypt. He is the founder of Christianity in Egypt.

I came out of Egypt both physically and spiritually. We left because as Christians we were persecuted. There is no freedom of speech in Egypt. Two government officials are assigned to every church to monitor what is being said. I was to work for the government as an architect. I graduated with honors in 1957, but I was passed by in promotion because my name is "Daniel," and to them it is a Christian name. The name keeps you from getting a higher job position. I worked for two hundred dollars a month. That is a salary of professional college graduates or even doctors.

I came to the United States in 1970 after 12 years' work as an architect with the Egyptian Government and because of my wife's health. She had open heart surgery for the mitral valve after which she developed severe asthma attacks. She had to use five or six pillows so she could sleep sitting up. The doctors in Egypt recommended she go to London or to the United States for the needed surgery to replace her heart valve.

A cousin of mine and his wife had gone to America. They were doctors in Shadyside Hospital in Pittsburgh. He said, "Come to the States. Stay with us. We will put your wife in the hospital, and they will operate."

Soon after we arrived, they set up a time for my wife's surgery. In the hospital, she was praying. She haphazardly opened the Bible to Jeremiah 33:3 (KJ). *"Call upon me, and I will answer thee, and show thee great and mighty things, which thou knowest not."*

She flipped to Mark 11:24 and read, *"What things so ever ye desire, when ye pray, believe that ye receive them, and ye shall have them."*

She prayed, "Lord, please take care of this operation. Help the doctor." She slept peacefully. During the night she saw a vision. Jesus came and touched her and said, "*I heal you from the top of your head to the bottom of your feet. You will not need the operation."*

The next day the doctor took her in to have an X-ray. To their amazement, they could find nothing wrong! They said, "Your blood pressure is good. Your cholesterol is good. Your valves are working good. Everything is good. What did you do? Did you have the operation already?"

"No. I was just praying last night. Jesus appeared. He touched me and said, '*You are healed. You don't need an operation.*'"

The doctor was Jewish. He said, "If you believe so, lady, it's all right with me. We'll keep you under supervision for three days. After that, we'll discharge you."

That miraculous healing in 1972 is recorded in Shadyside Hospital in Pittsburgh, PA.

When we first arrived in America, I looked for an architect position. I expected to get a job right away. Seventeen days passed, and I still didn't have work. My cousin gave us an apartment to live in until I found a job. I went to the American Institute of Architects. A lady gave me a list of architects who were busy in Pittsburgh.

Everywhere I went, they said I needed American experience. I finally said to one man, "How can I get American experience? I just came from Egypt! Here is my portfolio. This is what I did and can do. I worked in Saudi Arabia. I worked in Kuwait. I was in charge of the Asswan High Dam project."

The boss said, "Okay. We'll give you a chance."

I asked, "How much will you pay me?"

He said, "Three hundred and fifty dollars a week."

I thought, *My goodness!* Even a doctor or architect in Egypt is paid only two hundred dollars a month. I said, "I don't understand. You mean you're giving me three hundred and fifty dollars a week — or a month?"

He said, "A week. You are a graduate architect. Even that amount isn't enough, but we'll keep you under supervision for two years. If you do well, we will promote you after three months."

I couldn't believe this. It was three o'clock in the afternoon. I asked, "Can I start right away?"

"No. Come Monday morning."

I worked for the Polytech Company in Cleveland, Ohio. I was one of the team of sixty architects and engineers who designed the Gateway Stadium for the Cleveland Indians. Prior to that, I worked for twelve years for the Cafaro Co., in Youngstown, where I was involved in the design of malls around the States.

While working in Cleveland, I had friends in Akron, Ohio who opened their house for me to hold a Bible study with the Coptic Orthodox people. Through God's grace, twelve couples gave their lives to Christ. They learned the meaning of born again and made Christ the center of their lives. Praise the Lord!

In Egypt, I still have two married brothers. One is a doctor and another is a five-star general in the Egyptian Army. Since I accepted Christ as my Savior, I long to tell everyone about Him, whether they are from Egypt, India, or Israel.

In the States, I am an active member of the Gideon International. We distribute Bibles to hotels, motels, colleges, etc. At the beginning of last year we distributed 750 Bibles to freshmen at Thiel College, Greenville, PA. I praise the Lord for such a wonderful opportunity to serve the Lord in this capacity and reach out for the Lord through distributing God's Word.

Years ago, a friend of mine, a missionary from France, came to visit my wife and me. We were praying in our living room. All of a sudden, my wife was slain in the Spirit. She began to sing and speak in tongues.

I thought, *What is this?* I ran for a tape recorder and put it under the couch.

She sang in the Spirit for forty-five minutes. Finally, she said, "Thank God! Oh, praise the Lord!"

We felt as though we were in heaven. We could even smell incense in our living room. Our friend, a missionary for the Assemblies of God in France, missed his plane to Pittsburgh; but he was glad my wife had this experience. Later, I, too, received the Baptism of the Holy Spirit.

John 3:16 (NIV) reads, *"...whoever believes in him shall not perish but have eternal life."* This means anyone who humbly and sincerely opens his heart to Christ will receive the gift of eternal life by faith. The door is open to everyone as Christ said, *"He who comes to me I will in nowise cast out."*

I tell people about my experience: that if they have a fear of dying and going to hell, Christ can relieve them of their fear. They need to believe that Jesus is the Son of God, that He died on the Cross for us and rose again. Romans 10:9-10 says, *"If you confess with your mouth, 'Jesus is Lord,' and believe in your heart that God raised him from the dead, you will be saved. For it is with your heart that you believe and are justified, and it is with your mouth that you confess and are saved."*

I discovered when I asked God to forgive my sins, Jesus came into my heart and gave me joy and the peace that passes all understanding. This promise is found in I John 1:9 (NIV). *"If we confess our sins, he is faithful and just and will forgive our sins and purify us from all unrighteousness."*

I have no more fear. Jesus is mine. I have complete assurance of eternal life.

In I John 4:16-19 (NIV) we read, *"...God is love. Whoever lives in love lives in God, and God in him. In this way, love is made complete among us so that we will have confidence in the day of judgment, because in this world we are like him. There is no fear in love. But perfect love drives out fear, because fear has to do with punishment. The one who fears is not made perfect in love. We love because he first loved us."*

The joy of the Lord is my strength! (See Nehemiah 8:10)

Story as told to Barbara L. Michel

* * * * *

Dan Nasr can be reached at 724-981-7590 (Hermitage, PA) 16148.

Victory In Jesus

Barbara Michel

"Can you see me, Daddy?"

His blue eyes glistened with excess moisture. "No, Kitten. Daddy can't see anymore."

As a child this was a devastating blow; although it was not my initiation to blindness. Great *Grandmam* had been blind since before I was born. At ninety-two, she still baked scrumptious bread and sweet rolls. She did the dishes — except on Sunday. She said that was her day off. Great Aunt Rose, *Grandmam's* youngest daughter, lost her sight when she was fifteen. "Posey," as we called her, used to baby-sit with my siblings and me when we were little. She kept her house spotless, and her cooking was something worth going miles to enjoy. My father's mother had lost her sight, but she died before I was born.

Did the understanding of the capabilities of the blind soften the devastating blow of Daddy's not being able to see me again? No!

As the years progressed, I observed that the fruits of the Spirit, found in Galatians 5:22-23, were plentiful in my father's life. These are: *"love, joy, peace, patience, kindness, goodness, faithfulness, gentleness, and self-control."*

I had heard that the fruits of the Spirit were not only for oneself, but for those who were around us. I knew they were gifts of the Holy Spirit, but that each Christian must cultivate them. These fruits were evident in Daddy's faith in God, his positive attitude toward life, and in his relationship with others. From the time I was very young, I prayed, "God help me to follow Jesus and to pattern my life after my father's Christ-like example."

My older brother lost his sight about the same time as my father. My second brother's loss of sight soon followed. Both brothers seemed to resent their blindness, my second brother more than my first. This had the tendency to embitter him; true happiness evaded both.

Then came my challenge! In my late teens, I began to have trouble with my eyes. Glaucoma is a thief in the night. It creeps up like Satan to steal, kill, and destroy. *Why worry, though*, I thought. *Hasn't science made giant leaps toward solving glaucoma's black pit? Besides, there was more than enough blindness in the family. Jesus would not require me to live in the dark too, would He?* I prayed, believing that Jesus would not only touch my eyes and protect my sight, but that He would also return sight to others in my family.

Eye drops. Doctor's appointments. Surgeries. More doctor's appointments. Was there more to life than this? God could halt this downward spiraling? I believed and waited for my miracle.

The last surgery. The bandages removed. Darkness! I had joined the charcoal-gray world that my father and brothers were living in. At the time, I could still see shadows, confusing shapes, and blotches of distorted colors. Could I accept my circumstances as well as my father had? How? I was a landscape artist. My painting days were over. How could I stand this? What was I to do with the creative talent God had given me? Imprisoned, it stood gripping the bars of destiny. Reaching toward infinity, it discovered no immediate channel for artistic expression. Abominable frustration!

Jesus helped me. My path had crossed His before I was two years old. I knew, because one of the first things I remembered was that I loved Jesus and wanted to obey Him. I still did, more than ever; but would I be able to accept this stalemate and practice the fruits of the Spirit as my father did?

One of the verses I had learned in Bible school became a frequent thought. *"Do not be anxious about anything, but in everything, by prayer and petition, with thanksgiving, present your requests to God. And the peace of God, which transcends all understanding, will guard all your hearts and minds in Christ Jesus."* Philippians 4:6-7.

Even though my supplications to see were denied, I knew Jesus was with me and would give me strength to cope. God is faithful and He never breaks a promise. I found not only peace, but many new paths of expressions and witness. What about happiness? True joy is found in the Lord.

My mother continuously expressed, "Where there is a will, there is a way."

I believe, when it is God's will, He will show a way and be a constant encouragement.

Adjustments: Gerald and I had been married only a short time when blindness struck. He knew when we met that my continuing to see was in question; however, neither of us expected the dark cloud to descend so soon — or so fast. Gerald was in seminary. Although I had had a full-time job, I had read most of his theology books and typed his term papers. I was striving to be obedient to God's will and could not understand why He would let blindness happen. I could be a sightless wife; but what about being a minister's wife and accomplishing the parsonage and church responsibilities that were expected of one in that position? Aunt Posey could do it (actually, later in life, when she was in her fifties, she married a minister and managed very well. Before her wedding, she asserted that if Barbie can do it, I can, too.)

When blindness was still new to me, I prayed, "Oh, God, please help me pattern my life after your Son, Jesus Christ; empower me with your Holy Spirit, and give me the grace to accept my blindness and to endure as well as my father has. Give me strength and courage to obey Your Holy will."

Challenges struck. In August I had been driving a car; by September, I couldn't. I could see to get around when I went to the hospital for my fourth eye surgery. When I came home, it was near Christmas. All I could see were glowing spheres of defused colored lights on the tree. There had been no time to adjust. It was my first day home alone and in the dark; Gerald left early for classes. I stayed in bed, staring at the ceiling I could no longer see. There was a slight glimmer of light at the windows. That afforded little comfort. Sitting up, I took a deep breath. The only way God could help me to adjust was for me to accept my plight and to strive to be an overcomer. Could I? I didn't want to get up. I recalled a time in my early teens when I'd closed my eyes and tried to walk through the house like Daddy did. It was a disaster! I had little sense of direction and even less judge of distance. Now, my eyes are open. It makes no difference. *Now what, God?*

The thought, *Fear not for I am with you,* came to mind.

I figured that was easy for God to say. He wasn't the blind one! He was the supreme authority and Lord of my life though, so how could I doubt Him? Up and at it.

By the time Gerald came home, I had dinner ready. It was a simple meal of hamburgers, parsley potatoes, and canned peas. Other adjustments weren't as easy, by any stretch of the imagination; but with the Lord's gentle urging, I learned quickly. What hurt the most was the reaction of sighted people. Strangers gawked. Most Christians either silently pitied or overdid making me appear helpless, and it made me feel under-confident. Worse, friends no longer called. I was on a dark island, alone — except for God and my family. Was that enough? No. Why are so many sighted people so blind?

It took me a week or so to learn how to do the sundry household duties. First, I accomplished cooking. Laundry and cleaning followed. Gradually, the fragments of splotchy colors vanished; the glimmer of light faded to a dark gray mist; the oddly-shaped, flickering shadows disappeared.

At 21, I went to The Seeing Eye to get my first guide dog. Tammy was a wonder. We took daily walks and went for small grocery orders. My dog gave me independence and built my confidence. All the while, God was directing and encouraging.

The next January, Gerald accepted his first charge. I felt fortunate to have an appreciative husband. Since he had heavy church responsibilities, I spent much time alone. During the long days I discovered that, even though I could not see the notes to play the piano, God had given me a talent to play by ear. This was great!

Why do so many stereotype blind people? Is it because the only blind folks some know are the multiple handicapped, the mentally incapacitated, or the elderly who can no longer care for themselves — even if they had sight.

When Gerald's parents visited, they saw, believed, and appreciated my accomplishments. On one occasion at our first charge, Mom Michel came into the house huffing. She had discovered that one of the neighbors were of the opinion that Gerald accomplished his church duties and did the house work as well as taking care of his *poor* blind wife? Mom let me know that she had set the woman straight and in no uncertain terms!

Striving to prove my capabilities to almost everyone becomes wearisome. I continue to marvel at the apparent inability of the sighted to accept the potential of those who can't see. But, what about myself? Do I underestimate the abilities of persons who have other physical limitations? Heaven forbid! We should all pray for understanding and insight.

Elizabeth, our first baby, was born. Tongues wagged! Lips flapped behind my back like underwear in a brisk breeze. Excellent hearing made the whispers clear. "What's she going to do? How will she feed her baby? How will she bathe and change an infant? What will she do when she is home alone? That poor little baby."

Well, with God's help, I lived through the wagging and flapping. Overcoming the skepticism of people was a difficult challenge. I did a few things differently; but for the most part, I took care of my baby the same way as a sighted mother. I admit that my hearing became more acute.

Loni Lynn arrived the day before Elizabeth's second birthday. Christopher was born twenty-two months later. By this time I had ears that flicked at the slightest sound — much like those of a German Shepherd guide.

When my son was about seven, I heard one of his playmates coaxing him to come to his house to play. His argument went as follows. "When we're in another room, my mom doesn't know what we're playing with. *Your* mom knows what we're doing — even when we're upstairs!"

It pleased me, yet it made me wonder what it was that the little fellow wanted to get away with.

I prayed a lot for the safety of my children. When they were grown, my son asked how I had raised such great kids. I answered, "With a lot of prayer, blood, sweat, and tears, then a lot more prayer." Doesn't every Christian mother?

As the children grew, so did my church responsibility. This was a delight. I discovered that I could do as much in the dark as most ministers' wives did with sight. God was faithful. He blessed me with talents to replace the ones I could no longer use. In other instances, He showed me how to do a thing differently than I had done it with sight. This is victory from ashes; this is strength and courage endowed by the Holy Spirit. Praise the living God!

I had always loved music. That was one thing that did not have to change — well, much. I learned to play a guitar and started to lead youth groups and a youth choir. I formed a young adult singing group and did a lot of soloing. I think this ministry did almost as much for me as it did for those I ministered to. Preaching came next. It was a great joy to have gospel concerts and to hold evangelistic services.

At the end of my life, I want to be able to say as the

Apostle Paul has said, *"I have fought the good fight, I have finished the race, I have kept the faith."* II Timothy 4:7.

When Elizabeth was six, we discovered she had developed arrhythmia. At that time there was no way to correct her heart defect. Her life was in God's hands. We prayed for her healing and believed. How could we stand to lose her? God wouldn't give her to us, then take her, would He? That was one of the things I prayed about — often and in earnest.

God knows best — although, at times His actions are painful for us. When Elizabeth was thirteen, He took her home, quickly and without a warning that we understood. Shock. Disbelief. Unbearable grief. Then, the empowerment of the Holy Spirit. God lifted us up and gave us strength to cope, accept, and go on with life. If He wanted my little girl, I should be willing to give her back. After all, God sacrificed His only Son for me, and Jesus didn't die easily. He suffered agony and torture so that repentant mankind could live with Him eternally.

Elizabeth found her heavenly contentment quicker than the rest of us. The joy of the Lord was a balm for our sorrow. Does that mean we didn't grieve? No. Years later, there are sometimes tears. Elizabeth loved the Lord. She is not dead. She is with Christ. Someday, we'll see her again.

One way to relieve pain is to reach out to others who are suffering. After my experiencing the torment of losing a child, I counseled parents who had suffered similar losses and knew I'd understand their agony. Had this been God's reason for taking Elizabeth? I only know that God has promised that: *"In all things God works for the good of those who love him, who have been called according to his purpose."* Romans 8:28. He has promised to be with us and to never forsake us.

I desire to fulfill what God has planned for me; therefore, maybe I should expect the refining fire. Still, who among us is ready for the smelter?

In Psalm 139; 23-24, David wrote, *"Search me, oh God,*

and know my heart: test me and know my anxious thoughts. See if there is any offensive way in me, and lead me in the way everlasting."

I felt God's call to write, but as a minister's wife, there was no time; besides, I had nothing but a typewriter and no one to read my drafts. As the years marched forward, I felt the call stronger. Finally, I was able to schedule writing time, but having no computer posed a mountain of difficulties. With faith in the forefront, hope as my climbing gear, and the Lord's encouragement, I headed upward.

I had several articles published, wrote a column for a small national writer's magazine, and won two short fiction contests. Eventually God blessed me with a computer with a voice synthesizer that read back what I typed; therefore, I didn't need sighted help to make additions, deletions, or changes in the manuscript. At a later date I got a scanner that can read the print it scans. This brought research within my grasp. Modern technology is fantastic — as long as the electricity doesn't fail!

Gerald supported me and was a constant encourager. After seven years of sweat, my first novel was accepted and published. Two years later I have three novels in the EDEN series: SEARCH FOR EDEN, RETURN TO EDEN, and DAWN OF EDEN. BEYOND EDEN is the newest publication. Since this series has an Amish setting, the books have been accepted in tourist gift shops as well as Christian book stores. Recently a number of book stores in a large chain have asked for autographings. I praise God for the additional opportunities to speak in churches, schools, and writing conferences. Besides selling books, speaking engagements give me an opening to illustrate the capabilities of someone blind; more importantly, they are opportunities to witness to the Lord's power and grace. God is good.

Blindness is a challenge and a hardship, but not a complete handicap. Mobility is the main problem. If a blind person has a guide and a reader, as well as computer know-how, many doors are open. Obedience to God is foremost.

When we are in His will, He not only makes a way, but He guides us along the path. When we are tempest-tossed, Jesus gives peace in the midst of the storm.

In the future I hope to have more novels published. Among others, I have written two historical novels and one on spiritual warfare that I am praying earnestly to have accepted for publication. At differing times, these novels were accepted by three Christian agents. Each sent the manuscripts to publishers. They all said that, even though novels were excellently written, large Christian publishing houses were looking for big-name authors who had national connections. Still, I pray, hope, and wait for the Lord to move; however, not my will but His be done.

My responsibility is to obey and trust. God is ever faithful. It is more important to have Son-light, with controlled inner lighting than to see the light of the sun. Jesus said, *"I am the light of the world. Whoever follows me will never walk in darkness, but will have the light of life."* John 8:12.

No one that I know has ever asked for blindness, be it physical or spiritual. If there is no medical cure for physical blindness and one does not receive a miraculous healing, one must accept the situation and trust the Lord — that is, if one wants to experience joy in life. There is no excuse to be spiritually blind, for Christ freely offers salvation from that darkness. We are not alone. He helps us every step of the way.

We must do our part in the striving. Paul wrote, *"Not that I have already obtained this, or am already perfect; but I press on to make it my own, because Christ Jesus has made me his own. Brethren, I do not consider that I have made it my own; but one thing I do, forgetting what lies behind and straining to what lies ahead, I press on toward the goal for the prize of the upward call of God in Christ Jesus."* Philippians 3:12-14.

A strong faith in God and a solid Biblical theology, enhanced by a positive philosophy, gives strength to face each new crises. When we are zapped by one of life's unexpected and seemingly unfair situations, it is a test of faith and trust in God. With His encouragement, we must get up, clasp the hand He offers, and press on. Press on. Press on!

* * * * *

Barbara Michel can be contacted for ministry or her books from the Eden Series by writing to:
Praise Distributing
Box 3, 405 Maple Street
Hawthorne, PA 16230

Books from Barbara's Eden Series

From Bitter to Better

Ben Kinchlow

"Man, there she goes again!"

I didn't mind a bit when I had my tail to a crack and found my mother praying. It was OK. if I knew she was asking on my behalf, such things as, "Don't let my son get in trouble! Don't let them put him in jail! Don't let him get hurt!" Her words often got to me.

But she was just plain going too far when she started asking things like, "God, save my son! Bring him to church! Have him make Jesus Christ the Lord of his life!" Now, that kind of praying was far out!

I'd never say I was an atheist — I just never thought I'd get myself in a trap where I'd serve some God who really wasn't interested in me. Not for Mama; not for anyone.

For the most part I felt that God had the things He wanted to do — I had my things, and never the twain could meet. If God would stay out of my way — I'd stay out of His!

Mama had dared to be a "born-again Christian" for a good many years, but I didn't see any reason for me to join her. I somehow got the idea that joy and fun and having a good time in life didn't mix with Christianity. I couldn't see how you could do all the fun things in life and still be a Christian.

The Christians I knew for the most part didn't seem very

Photo by Joe Lust

happy. They looked miserable and poor. Most of the time they were sick. As far as I could see, they seldom had anything going for them except dying and I wasn't for that. The only difference was Christians sneaked around doing all the things I did openly. Why sneak?

I grew up in a small southwestern town in Texas; consequently, in life, I came up against racial prejudice, but I didn't know what it really was until I got ready to go away to high school. All through elementary and junior high, I had gone to a school close to my home with my friends. I didn't even know it was segregated. I never wanted to truck up to the other side of town with a bunch of white kids. I never realized I *COULDN'T* go up there! I just thought the school I was attending was the place to go!

When I graduated from the eighth grade, I discovered they wouldn't *LET* me go to the town high school! It is very difficult for a young person to understand that the only reason he can't do something is because he was made different.

Well, how was I different? My skin was a different color. Look around you — people have blue eyes and blond hair or grey or brown hair, but people don't discriminate against them on account of that. I couldn't help the color of my skin anymore than you can determine the real color of your hair. Now, I know some of you ladies can change your hair color these days, but there just wasn't anything I could do to alter the color of my skin.

I had the darnedest time trying to figure out why people wanted to punish me for something I didn't have anything to do with and that was impossible to change.

Who made me this color? God! That was one strike against Him. I just blamed Him for all the problems I was having with the people because of my color.

I'll tell you something, man, when a young person is growing up he needs to have a positive self image. If somebody doesn't continually tell him, "You're valuable — we love you — you're a human being with dignity and worth," he begins to develop a negative self-image and, consequently, has to do something to enable him to accept himself.

A lot of young kids get into drugs and alcohol because they are looking for something to help them cope. When young guys feel they can't face reality on their own because they don't think they have any value or worth, they start taking a couple of hits of dope, smoking pot, or drinking booze to make themselves feel more like men.

That's why I started drinking — that's why I started smoking. I wanted to feel like somebody — like I was a real tough customer. Still — inside I was scared to death. I didn't want anybody else to know that, so I had to find some way to deal with that feeling.

I went to a Catholic high school and found that Catholics, bless their hearts, have a tendency to think they have the only true religion. Now, all of us Baptists and Methodists know that's not the truth — we have the true religion! Ha!

The tendency of the Catholics is to feel that you're bound for hell if you aren't Catholic. We had nuns who were fine teachers. They told me about the church, religion, the sacraments, the mass — but nobody told me about Jesus! Nobody ever told me that I could have a personal relationship with Jesus Christ!

I am not condemning the Catholic Church — I have heard Pentecostals, Baptists, Methodists, and Presbyterians who feel just as strongly about their religious persuasion. They all feel the Catholics are going to hell!

The Catholics impressed me, though. They seemed more serious about their religion than the Baptists and Methodists. At least the Catholics went to church every morning. You wouldn't find a Baptist going to services every day. Even if they claimed not going to church was a mortal sin — they just didn't go!

If you got a Baptist out on Sunday morning and Sunday night and got him back on Wednesday night for prayer meeting — you had a real committed Christian there! The

Catholics went every morning, man! And they made me go the whole time I was in high school. That must have counted for something even though I almost always slept through most of the mass.

When I got out of high school, I joined the service. All of a sudden I was faced with the military and needed something comforting, so I went back to the familiar. I joined the Catholic church. It gave me a sense of belonging. No matter where I was sent, then — I knew I would feel as though I belonged some place.

I wasn't a very good Catholic. I stayed in the church thirteen years. In the meantime I was stationed in many overseas areas. Among the things I found out was that all my life I'd been taught a fallacy. I'd always been told that I was part of a minority. People said that black people were a minority, black people were inferior, and the reason for segregated schools was because black people just couldn't compete with everybody else.

When I got overseas, I saw the black people over there were not the minority. Just the opposite. In fact, the more I traveled outside my own country, the more I found out that the *WHITE* people were the *MINORITY,* not the so called "colored" people!

That really revolutionized my thinking. I thought, *"WOW!* Put enough of us together — we can get rid of you all. There's more of us than the rest of you!"

That was my kind of thinking then. At that time a sort of nationalism began to rise among the various nations around the world — a move to kick out the "white imperialists." It was a strange thing to walk down the street in the Dominican Republic or Puerto Rico where the people who looked just like me would yell, "Yankee Imperialist — go home!!"

I didn't consider myself a Yankee Imperialist. The white people were the imperialists, and I just happened to be in the military. Yet they were telling me to go home!

That was a weird feeling, man. A feeling of nationalism — a sense of pride in my race began to swell within me. I started finding all kinds of black people in black history that went back years and years. Cleopatra was black and Solomon must have been a black man.

Some people say that Jesus had to be black! When you look at people in that part of the world — and I was in that part of the world in the Middle East — it is very difficult to visualize anyone in that area with blond hair and blue eyes or light brunette hair or very pale skin. Besides, Jesus spent most of his time out in the sun. When you see those people over there, it seems natural to decide that Jesus was dark brown.

The big thing that kind of swelled my bad feelings was the episode at Little Rock, Arkansas. While I was stationed overseas, people at home were trying to segregate the Little Rock school system. And I remember, man, that there I was with the U.S. military uniform on my back and having sworn an oath to protect and defend the Constitution of the United States and the American way of life — if it cost me my very own life — and there they were, showing me, while I was still overseas, the television coverage of the Little Rock situation.

With unbelieving eyes, I saw scenes of the National Guard — other men in uniform — with fixed bayonets pointed to prevent eight little black children from getting into an American high school. And I had sworn to protect this with my life!

I thought, "Man, something's rotten in Denmark! Something's not right here!" It was at that point my allegiance to America began to go down hill. I started to get bitter.

I was supposed to be angry with the Communists, but no Communist was denying me access to the things the Constitution guaranteed me!

Then my mole hills started growing into mountains. Small things started festering inside of me. Can you imagine taking your little boy by the hand into an American department store with American money in your pocket — you, an American in an American uniform with your little son — to buy American merchandise in this American place of business. You walk up to the counter to pay, and your little boy looks up at you and says, "Daddy, I have to go to the potty!"

"Hey, great!" you think. "The boy's learning. No more messes in his pants!"

You put a smile on your face and ask the clerk, "Where's the rest room?"

Her face freezes as she answers, "We don't have restrooms for colored in here."

What are you supposed to do in a case like that? Are you going to smile and tell your little boy, "No problem, son. Just hold it till we get outside!"?

When this kind of thing happens over and over, you start getting bitter and unhappy and looking for places to get revenge. You think, "It's everyone's fault — not just southern folks' fault!"

That's part of what's wrong with young people today. That's why in the sixties there were so many banks blown up. They were looking for ways to lash out and that's the way it was with me. My spirit of rebellion began to build higher.

I thought, "I'm getting out of the service and I'm going to fight my real enemy — the white man!" A group called the Black Muslims were just coming on the scene, and they were telling us, "Unite and get the white people off your neck. Remember, you're somebody and you can be proud of who you are."

I got into that rhetoric. I didn't have much else to hang on to, so I got into that. The next thing you know I was ready to shave my head and change my name to "X" and go out and start doing what I thought I had to do.

The guy who really impressed me was the dude called Malcolm X, but he got killed before I could realize my ambition to join up with him. Then I heard a lot of stuff about a guy who claimed to be the spiritual leader of the nation of Islam. But I heard rumors that he had gotten some secretary pregnant in Chicago, and I thought, "Oh, man, another dude who's ripping off the people."

After that I just kind of fell away from everything except my determination to change the circumstances of the black person. I decided to go back to college. I knew from being in the Air Force that it didn't matter how right your cause was — you could be yelling, *"BLACK POWER AND BROWN POWER OR BOYCOTT POWER,"* but if you didn't have some *GREEN POWER to* back it up — your revolution would pretty soon come to a screeching halt!

I went back to college because I knew that the people in this country who had educations could make big money, and big money taught the poor people what to do. If you had money, you could pay people to do almost anything. You could buy guns, you could buy demonstrators, you could buy people if you only had enough money.

So I thought, "I'm going to get enough money so that I won't have to be out there on the streets marching up and down and carrying a sign saying, *"WE SHALL OVERCOME!"*

I had a very bad habit when I was a kid — if people hit me — I hit back. If I were walking down the street and someone hit me on my head, I would not turn around and sing to him, "We shall overcome."

I'd be real overcome, all right — I'd take that sign and bat him over the head. That's the way I felt about the whole thing!

I heard preachers preach, "Love the white people. Don't hate the white people. If thy neighbor smite thee on one cheek, turn the other cheek."

I said, "Man, the white folks don't believe that, even if they are Christians. And if you don't believe me, you go to any church in America and walk down front and find some deacon with his hair all slicked back sitting there all dignified and smelling of Old Spice, and walk right up with your big Afro and your shades and your fu Manchu mustache and say, *"BROTHER"* and go *BOP* in his face.

He's not going to turn and smile, "The Lord bless you, my brother." No, man!

That pretense was a white man's lie to keep Christians in bondage, that's all it was! They tried to shove a white Jesus down my throat! If they had a white Jesus they must have had a white God. They never saw a black angel. They never saw anybody black associated with the Bible.

Can you imagine? Here are some people who won't even let me in the rest room with them. Then they turn around and claim that there's One of them who knows every stinking, rotten thing I ever did. *HE'S* going to lay down *HIS* life for *ME?* Are you kidding? You really didn't expect me to believe that, did you?

Oh, come on, man, I told myself, you'd have to be a fool to believe that a white man who wouldn't let you in his church on Sunday nor sit beside you on a bus is going to deliberately give HIS life for YOU? Come on!

I can't lie about it — that's the way I felt. My life was pretty rugged. I'll tell you something about hatred. Hatred doesn't just start out where you're aiming. Hatred doesn't destroy the people you point it at. Hatred begins to destroy YOU. It begins to destroy your family, your mental stability; you start to get ulcers.

First, you only hate white people; but after a while you even begin to hate brown people — Mexicans, in addition to white Anglo-Saxon Protestants. I began to hate them because they acted like they thought they were white.

And then I got to a point where I even hated other blacks if they didn't agree with me. If one didn't say I was right, I called him "Uncle Tom" and hated him. After a while I got where I was hating my family because they weren't doing what I thought they ought to do. But most of all — I hated *ME!* Underneath I really knew that the problem was me, but I didn't know what to do about it!

After you live long enough, you have to realize that you can only blame somebody else for your problems for so long and then you have to come up with something better and that's why kids get all strung out on drugs or alcohol or whatever. When the truth finally dawns, "It's really my fault

— it's not somebody else's" — you begin to say, "Wow! I really am a loser!" You start to try to find some way to cover up your own inadequacies.

So I began to hate myself. I didn't really believe I was inadequate, but I didn't know where else to turn.

I was breaking up with my wife and family because they couldn't please me. Everything was going down hill. On the outside I looked successful. I was a part-time salesman as well as a college student. I was an "A" student, high on the dean's honor roll, was president of my class, taught a karate course, had a black belt in karate, and drove test cars at night.

Because of all my activity I knew I was fairly successful in the world's eyes. Besides, I was making about twelve thousand dollars a year. Thirty-two years ago, before inflation got so bad, twelve thousand dollars was a lot of money for a college student working part-time.

"I've got it made, man! I know where I'm going! I'm successful! We've got a new car, a nice home. Don't have any bills. We're doing real good!" Those were the things I kept telling myself.

Except, we weren't. Nothing was good at home! One day I drove there and loaded my king-sized bed on a borrowed pickup and drove off because I'd had it! Fighting, arguing, squabbling — my home was my battle camp. My wife and I had little truces going — sometimes we'd call a short truce to talk to each other, but the rest of the time we didn't communicate at all.

When I did talk to my kids — I yelled. I yelled at my wife. I never talked to my family — I yelled at them. I began to develop an ulcer. Then my marriage broke completely. I filed for divorce. I was finished - through!

Then I met this guy who was exactly the opposite of everything I thought you should be. People said you had to be successful, you had to have a college education, you had to have a goal, you had to have a plan, you had to be achieving all the time.

Not this character, man. He was the exact opposite. He

didn't have a college degree, nor did he intend to get one. He didn't have any 'goals' so to speak — he didn't plan to be making fifty thousand dollars a year at age thirty-five. He didn't have a whole lot of money; he wasn't even trying to get any! Man, was he strange! He wasn't like the rest of us — there had to be something wrong with him!

I kept looking at him and wondering what made him tick. When you find somebody strange — too strange — you keep asking around, "Hey, what's with that dude over there?"

When someone said, "He's a preacher," the thought crossed my mind, "that figures." Preachers were strange dudes most always. But! This one wasn't preaching like any preacher I ever knew. He wasn't always grabbing someone and telling him to repent or come to church or whatever!

He walked around like he really cared about his people — like they were the most important things in his life. Whatever they talked about and thought was important — he listened to! I couldn't believe it!

You find very few preachers who listen, very few Christians who listen. Christians are geared up to witness and witness means hitting people with the three spiritual laws, getting them to their knees and then chalking them up on a spiritual tote board. Then you can hit the road and brag, "Another convert — I got another one!" Just like counting sheep.

But this guy didn't push like this. To my surprise I found myself pouring out my heart and soul to this dude. All the hangups, all the inhibitions came rolling out of my mouth. I found myself spilling my guts because I had finally found someone who cared and would listen.

When I spilled the beans to this guy, I told him all my notions about God. He knew my past feelings about Jesus. Too many people are like I had been — with too many preconceived ideas about Him. In some cases the feelings were not negative like mine, but the downfall of such people happened because of their religious concepts of what God is like — of what Jesus is like.

"Jesus can do certain things. God can do certain things. God can't do certain things because my religion preaches that God can't do them." When we say and believe that, we limit God!

We all have preconceived notions about the Lord. Just like my ideas had me trapped - other people's beliefs have them trapped. I began to let go of many of these notions about God as I watched this guy's life.

My own life had been something else before I met John Cochran. One night while I was driving one of the test cars, I began thinking over one of the things he had told me: "Ben, you might not realize it, but the Lord has been watching over you for years. Someday I'm sure you'll have to acknowledge that."

Scenes from my past suddenly flooded my mind. I could have been in jail. I could have lost my life in a gun battle with a guy the time I went to kill him. The only reason I wasn't killed was because somebody saw me coming to him when he had a pistol in his belt and closed the door between us. He wanted to kill me, too, and I didn't know he had a pistol at the time. If I'd have stepped out in front of him, he would have shot me dead.

The only reason that I'm not in the penitentiary for killing is because I went another time with my pistol, the safety off, and my hand on the trigger, and knocked at the guy's door, he wasn't there!

If he had opened that door, I would surely have killed him. That's just the way it was. But he wasn't there, and I know now he wasn't supposed to be. I'd gone to the desk clerk and got his room number, but he wasn't inside. If he had opened the door — if anyone had opened it — right or wrong guy — he'd have been dead!

Another time I was in a car accident. My best friend and I were together. He got wiped out just like that, but I went through the back window, and bounced down the median strip. The car turned over three or four times, and all I got was a slight scratch on the arm. That accident killed my friend, but not me. Why not me?

"My Heavenly Father Watches Over Me." The words of a song from my childhood echoed and re-echoed through my mind. I thought, "Maybe John Cochran is right! God, I've seen his life. I've watched my mother praying for me all these years."

I guess, for the first time in my life, I was honest with God. "God," I said. "I don't really know if You're out there."

Now, don't think I never prayed to Him before. When you got yourself in a tight mess, you pray, "God, if You just get me out of this mess, I'm not going to do this anymore." You're serious — dead serious — at the time you say all this. At that particular point when the pressure was on and I didn't know where to turn, I was always serious. But as soon as God got me out of hot water, and not being born-again, I went back to my same old habits and started doing the same old things over again. Sometimes I went along as much as three days, but then I went back to my old self again.

There in the test car was the first time I came to Him when I wasn't in a panic, nor was I emotional.

I had to be honest. "God," I repeated, "I really don't know if you are there." I'd heard a lot of talk about Jesus Christ, but I didn't know who Jesus was so I said, "If you're really out there and Jesus Christ really is who You say He is — Your Son — then, if You can — do something with my life."

Then I paused. "Wait a minute — if all You've got to offer is religion — if I have to be religious —- You can keep that. I don't need religion!"

Now, I want to tell you, man, Jesus Christ is *REAL!* He is the Son of God! God Almighty rules right now. He sits on a real throne in a real place in heaven.

I know, for Jesus Christ, in answer to that prayer, came down and revealed Himself to me. I didn't see somebody standing out in the middle of a field — no bright lights started flashing, no great bells were ringing or angelic choirs singing. But, all of a sudden, a certain quiet knowledge filled me. "Hey, He really *IS!*"

The only thing I could say then was, *"WOW! I'm sorry!"*

What else could I say, except "I'm sorry. If You can do anything with my life, please change me!" It was a plea from my heart, for I suddenly had that heart knowledge that told me "He's for real!"

I want to tell you, man, Jesus came into my life, and I didn't know anything then about Second Corinthians 5:17 — *"If any man be in Christ, he is a new creature."*

I didn't know the Bible said that! I didn't know it said, *"All things pass away and old things become new."* I knew nothing about that at all because people had just told me about "religion." Jesus Christ came into my life. He took away all the hatred, the bitterness, the self-hatred. I could love my wife again—I hadn't been able to get along with her for so long. I could love my kids—they weren't those rotten little beasties anymore. They were my children, and I could love them like my Heavenly Father could love me!

I could love white people! They weren't white people anymore; they were just people. Suddenly I discovered I was color blind. I didn't know what color people were and cared less!

More than that—I didn't need somebody else's approval to be accepted, and I didn't need to do anything to be accepted!

There is no way to explain to anyone who has never met Jesus Christ what it means to be clean. That's the only way I can think of to tell you how it is. I was washed clean by His blood and became a brand new person in Christ Jesus. I even began to like *ME!*

Seven months later I found a passage of scripture, John 8:31,32. *"If you continue in My Word, you will be disciples indeed and the truth will set your free."* That was the truth—Jesus made me free and I've grown ever since.

For many years I was affiliated with the 700 Club as a co-host on the show. The Lord has richly blessed me since I gave my life to Him. My life story "Plain Bread" has been a best-seller. The work I feel the Lord has put on my heart is to tell everyone regardless of their status in life — rich or poor — black or white — sick or healthy — that they are special and Jesus loves them.

* * * * *

At the time of this writing, there is an ominous sound of potential danger in the distance. The danger has a name, and a drop-dead date for arrival — the "millennium bug," or "Y2K."

In my opinion, we should follow the admonition of the Lord Jesus Christ to be as wise as serpents and as harmless as doves; trusting that God knows how to make a difference for His people.

We can take comfort in His provision for Israel in the midst of the plagues striking Egypt. With this in mind, we should take prudent steps to ensure that we are prepared for three to six months of possible difficulty.

My first suggestion is to try to have three to six months of operating capital in cash; in a safe place in your home, or in a safety deposit box. I anticipate that there will be some bank closures if fear gets out of hand.

I also suggest ensuring that you have adequate purification means to provide drinking water for your family. Bleach (as directed), boiling, and certain water purifiers are recommended. You should also try to provide subsistence-type rations, which can be consumed with a minimum of preparation. I would recommend three to six months supply per family member.

Finally, a reliable power source should be secured. A diesel generator that would enable you to run essential services such as heat, emergency lighting, etc. For additional information, you may like to check Y2K sites especially www.teamnetinternational.com.

I am not a pessimist, nor am I a Pollyanna. I believe that God will protect, but as Shadrach, Meshach, and Abednego said to Nebucadnezzar, *"Our God whom we serve is able to deliver us, but if not, we will not bow down to your gods."* Let us not allow fear and misunderstanding to cause us to turn away from our faith in *"Him, who is able to do exceedingly above all we can ask, or think, by the power that is at work within us."*

For information contact Ben Kinchlow's office in Chesapeake, VA.

War - Then Peace

Dr. Peter J. Wasko

As a kid no one told me what to do. My mother and father got divorced, and Mom remarried when I was about thirteen. My step-father, Ben, never tried to discipline me because I wasn't his.

Back at the age of eleven, I started drinking. By the time I was seventeen, my brother squealed on me for being drunk all the time. Mom and Ben, in desperation, told me, "We're going to have to ground you." No one was going to tell ME what to do, so I quit school and joined the Army.

On my eighteenth birthday, while I was stationed in Germany, I received a gift package in the mail. Anticipating its contents, I tore it open, only to find of all things - a BIBLE! The name "Peter Wasko" was engraved on the cover. I'll never forget that present as long as I live. It came from my mother— who wasn't a Christian!

When I was quite young, Mom and I used to sit in our little apartment and read all the red lettering in scriptures since we at least knew they were supposed to be the words of Jesus.

I'd ask her, "What does this mean?" when I came to things I couldn't comprehend. Sometimes we'd both get so frustrated that we'd wind up crying. My mother couldn't answer my questions about how the Bible related to life because she didn't know what to say. At that point she simply didn't understand.

The Bible came in the mail just at the time the Army was in the process of trying to kick me out. They had me going to a psychiatrist. I decided to take my new black book to the Catholic priest and the Baptist and Methodist chaplains asking, "What do you think this means?" - "What's your explanation for this?" These good men didn't know how to answer me. They just told me what they'd been taught, but none of them seemed to have a grasp on the real meaning of God's Word. Since it didn't seem to be alive to them, they came across as spiritually dead.

Since I knew that the Army was trying to decide how to get rid of Pete Wasko, I volunteered for Vietnam. They sent me to what we called "Dumb-dumb school" for a week. I volunteered for another week of demolition training.

At the age of eighteen I was a trained killer qualified to use various weapons and detect, disarm, and set up booby traps. They even taught me how to sever someone's head! In my mind, Pete Wasko became a hot shot. All that knowledge thrilled me. I'd grown up in a low-income neighborhood, and I'd had to learn how to fight and defend myself when I was small.

If I was going to Vietnam, I wanted to see some real action. No sir, I was no pansy! I'd seen all the John Wayne movies, — "Pork Chip Hill" and that kind of stuff. I was ready to go - ready to fight.

When I arrived in Vietnam, I was classified as a "Recon Scout." After two weeks the word came ordering us out on our first ambush patrol. Action, at last!

Thoughts that passed through my mind that day are etched in my mind forever. As we moved out, I was the next-to-the-last guy. I thought, *"If they get the last guy, they'll probably get the next one in line."* That was Pete Wasko, and believe me, he was scared to death!

Once we got into position, we were told, "You'll each stand guard for two hours, then you can sleep for the next two."

This is my first ambush patrol and I'm suppose to sleep? Get real! I knew I was going to be up all night. At two in the morning, when I'd rousted my buddy Larry up to take over the watch for enemy action, I told him, "Whatever you do - DON'T fall asleep!"

While lying there thinking, fear swept over me. *"What if the enemy steals up and gets him with a knife?* Other thoughts that raced through my mind were phenomenal - *"Where's base camp from here?"*

"Miller?" I whispered hoarsely into the night. No answer! *Was he dead? Is there a 'Gook' lying low waiting for me? What am I going to do?*

I crawled over toward Miller. The men were scattered about twenty feet away from each other. Right up beside his face, I whispered "Miller!" again. His eyes were closed. Was he dead?

"What? What? What?" he cried as he came to. He was sleeping! I wanted to kill him myself - I was so mad!

Even though I didn't know it then, that night changed my sleep habits for the next nineteen years. I was afraid to go to sleep for that long because I might die in my sleep as a result of somebody else's mistake.

I snarled into the night, "I'm not going to turn you in. I'm not going to get you court marshaled, but you're mine next time! I'm not going to die because somebody else is sleeping!" For the next nineteen years, Satan used that scare to keep me from ever letting my guard down and getting rest.

A week later they shipped us off to the field. As a gunner on an armored personnel carrier, I was under a sergeant who was serving his third tour of duty in Vietnam. He'd been wounded eight times and had five stars - three silver and two bronze. To me he was an Audie Murphy. He just loved being there. I respected this man even though I'd seen him in action a couple of times when he'd accidentally killed a couple of people.

When we were at mail-call, some little lambrettas (You've

seen them in the Oriental movies - they look like little jeeps) went by while we were sitting on a piece of equipment with a 50-caliber machine gun and 3,000 pounds of ammunition inside. At that moment this other guy had an M-16, and he pulled the trigger to see if it was cocked or not. The thing went off. My sarge thought the gunfire came from the lambrettas, so he swung around and fired. In an instant he'd killed everybody there! He blew them away before they ever had time to think. I didn't know what was going on! All I knew after that was I wanted to be close to my sergeant. This guy was never going to go to sleep on me!

With a sense of awe and respect, I went on a search and destroy mission. While we were out there, he asked, "Pete, do you smoke?'

"Yep!" I answered.

"How long have you been smoking?"

"Since I was about eleven."

He looked at me and smiled as he handed me a bowl full of weed and said, "You've never had any like this before."

In my mind I thought, *I meant cigarettes*, but he'd handed me dope! What was I supposed to do? This is someone I really, really respect.

Prior to that I'd have turned anyone in who I caught smoking dope. I didn't care who they were.

I thought, *this dope stuff's all in your mind anyway,* so I started to drag on it and I didn't notice any difference. It wasn't until after I'd smoked it three or four times that I realized it was in my mind, but in a way I never imagined. It had caused me to have a different persepective of what was going on.

We got a call to move our unit a little farther north on the Cambodian border in a village called Locnina. There a small unit of Green Berets was holding a landing zone.

We heard from headquarters that there was some enemy activity in the area. On our way up we were part of a convoy that was being mortared from the tree lines. This was our first time to face such action. There you are, driving down the road, when all of a sudden, you would see a small puff of smoke from the tree line and a little hollow sound like the tubes being used to set off fireworks. Then a bomb went off. Up to this point, I had thought that Vietnam was kind of neat. There hadn't been anyone wounded except the enemy.

Once we got to where there was a French plantation, we were in steady contact at least once a day for twenty-two days in a row. There I was — eighteen years old and hadn't been in Vietnam for a month, when we were engaged in fire-fighting. A lot of times during a fire-fight, we didn't see anything but a wild, bright, noisy display of fire power.

The day things changed for me was when we got two prisoners, and the prisoners were put on the same APL we were on. I was sitting on the back deck of this vehicle, and the adrenaline was pumping. Man, was it going through me! As a recon scout, I was allowed to carry a MP-45, and I had a M-60 machine gun. Both of the prisoners were standing across from me, and I could see them first-hand. The next thing I know, our commander, who is a sergeant, puts a vice grip around one of their necks and brutally does him in.

As I listened to their screams, I thought, *What's going on?* My thinking was thrown off-kilter. That was the second time I ever saw anyone get killed or die. The only time I'd ever seen anyone dead was at a funeral home. I was shaken to the bone!

I looked around, and I saw that I was the only one upset with this horror. Everyone else was desensitized to the atrocity we'd witnessed. They acted as though the sarge had just stepped on an ant or something. *Oh, God,* I cried inside. *What's happening? Is this for real?*

The whole episode had its impact on me. The next thing I knew I was shooting at every little movement around me. I was scared to death!

They called us into a little meeting one night to tell us about our mission for the next day where we were to be engaged in combat with at least one thousand Vietnamese. Our job was to pull them out in the open. When they opened fire on us, we were to call an air strike in on them. *Fifty against a thousand!* I thought. The odds were against us. We knew that before we started.

What am I going to do about this, God? How am I going to get out of this mess? There is no way out of this nightmare! Do I want to be tagged as a coward and be sent home? At least I'd be alive, but how do I deal with being called "coward"? Do I go on this suicide mission?

As we went toward our destination, there was a spotter plane in front of us. His message didn't help my fears, "The enemy's in front of us and they're spreading out."

The next thing I knew, there was a loud crack, and the guy next to me had his head taken right off. The other two were killed. From then on, everything was a mess. The battle was over in fifteen or twenty minutes; but before it ended, we'd expended almost all our ammunition.

They'd come in waves, and I'd been shooting point-blank into the oncoming enemy. What else could I do? Each one of our vehicles had expended almost all of our ammo, and we were down to the last. Our captain had just called in the air strike when he got shot right through the stomach.

An awesome panic overwhelmed us until we looked in the sky and must have felt like the guys in the old movies when the cavalry came over the hill. The jets were coming!

They dropped napalm all around us. You could see it burning everyone and everything on the earth. The Vietnamese dead was said to be over 1,100 when it was over, and another 1,000 were running back into Cambodia.

We had to get the vehicles out of that jungle at night. The artillery unit walked us out of the jungle using alumination rounds. No ammo had been dropped. We felt like illuminated bulls-eyes on a target.

After that, I didn't even trust the government, the enemy, or anyone but a few of the guys around me who were in the same shoes. I began shooting at everything until

Tommy, my closest buddy, pulled me down, smacked me and said, "Pete, snap out of it. We're gonna be okay. We came together; we're going home together."

I snapped out of it. Later, when we were going into a village, the "Gooks" had us in a U-shape ambush. The village we were protecting opened up on us as well. As we were trying to evacuate our wounded, a rocket-propelled grenade hit a tree beside us; and I was sprayed in the head and hand with shrapnel. Heat flooded my head and hand and I was covered with blood. I looked in a mirror, and I saw shrapnel sticking out of my head. I got up and started shooting again! The sad part of it was - I never thought of a Vietnamese person as a human; to me, they were simply "Gooks."

After that, they sent us off to an area we called "Holiday Inn." Since I wasn't married or didn't realize how many people really cared for me at home, and it didn't matter to me if I lived or died, I started to volunteer for all the married men's missions. Yet, I still carried my little black Bible.

In John 15:13 I read that there was no greater thing to do than to lay down your life for your friends. So I said, "Well, God, since I'm going to die and go to hell anyway, maybe ..." I was trying to bargain with God for my soul, even though I didn't understand the Bible or the Lord or its principles.

Then my buddy, Tom, went on an R&R in Hawaii to see his wife. When he returned, he asked, "Pete, can I talk to you?" I agreed, but he broke down and started to sob as he said, "I just saw my wife for the last time. I'm going to die"

As his weeping got out of control, I grabbed my friend and shook him, "Tom! Tom! Remember when you told me that we came here together, and we're going home together? We still are!"

"Pete, I can't let you go on my missions anymore. Something inside tells me not to let you go. I have to go myself. I told my wife this, too."

After we talked for a couple of hours, we got a call to

take the infantry out to an enemy base camp we found, and we were to secure it till morning.

I told Tom, "You stay here."

"No, I'm going, Pete."

Within a half hour, Tom was dead. When I got the word, I was so upset and angry that I couldn't contain myself. The guy I'd been willing to lay down my life for was gone!

He had a family. I thought I had nothing. *Okay, God, You're going to pay for this one,* I thought. *I'm going to become Satan's right-hand man.*

I took His scripture verses and turned them into mine. "Do unto others before they have a chance to do unto you." "Vengeance is mine saith Pete Wasko."

Every time I went out on patrol, I made sure there were no enemy survivors. I defied the Lord, "God, what are you going to do to me? You put them together — I'm taking them apart!"

Four days after Tom was killed, we hit a land mine which we were told held at least 100 pounds of dynamite. I was right on top of it. The impact blew a hole four-foot in diameter right through a mine shield, and my buddies said I was blown 60 feet in the air! When I landed, I thought both my legs were torn completely off. A guy named Gary Johnson ran back to me, "Are you okay, Pete?"

He said, "Your legs are intact, but you have some shrapnel in your face." Glancing down, I saw my body was covered with blood. Gary put my head between my knees. Within ten minutes I was up and walking. They flew me to the hospital and stitched my chin, but I was filled with hate and revenge.

After being in the hospital for three days, I found I was having a hard time walking. Because of being blown so high and landing so hard, my body wasn't functioning right. But a couple of weeks later, I was madder than a hornet and wanted revenge.

With a brand new APC unit, I was ready to fight again. The crazy part was - I was never mad at the Vietnamese - I was always mad at God. All my buddies that I had been volunteering for kept getting killed when I wasn't around.

On another beautiful sunny day, we'd picked up a couple of prisoners. As I turned around, another land mine went off. That time, I can remember I never blacked-out. When I came down on the top of the APC, I was on my hands and knees. Ammunition was blowing up all around me. I crawled over the edge and fell down into a pool of blood. My driver came and pulled me under a tree to keep the boiling hot sun off me. Everyone kept saying, "The chopper's on its way. Pete, you're gonna be okay."

My main concern as I looked around is that all five guys were intact. Metal was embedded in the side of my head; my knees were balloons. My back was hurt so I couldn't stand up.

All my concerned friends were asking what they could do, and I couldn't believe what came out of my mouth. This animal - Pete Wasko - said, "Lets say the Lord's Prayer together."

As we started to pray, everyone was weeping, sobbing, and crying. Not one person died, including the two POW's we'd captured!

I don't know how long I was in the hospital that time because I was on drugs. One day I remember they brought some of our wounded in with some Vietnamese Gooks alongside GI's! Horrified, I realized that the medics had to try to save them too.

When I came home from Nam, I was a basket-case. The emotional scars were on my mind forever and ever. My first assignment back in the states was to guard Vietnam Vets that couldn't adapt to being in the States, and my second assignment was to bury GI's who were killed in Vietnam.

As soon as I left the Army, I went to Youngstown State University so that I could be a registered nurse. In class the political science professor started talking about how guys were crazy for going to Vietnam and dying for no reason. I got up and walked out.

He followed me. I grabbed him by the neck and threw him against the wall and snarled, "I'm one of those crazy Vietnam Vets you're talking about!" He went back inside. I never went back to his class, but he passed me.

A few days later I wound up in a mental institution in Pittsburgh, PA, because I'd been walking down the street punching out windows. They had me in a straight jacket, but I had no idea how long I'd been there.

My heart goes out to people in mental wards because I've felt their hurts. I remember they took me out of this padded cell and took off my straight jacket and put me in front of a group of doctors. One asked, "Pete, do you know where you are?"

"I guess I'm in a hospital somewhere."

"You're in a nut house."

When he said that, I came out of the chair, grabbed him by the neck, and started choking him. People were screaming. I felt my pants come down and I felt a stab. Lights our for Wasko!

I have no notion how long I was out; but a few days later, they got me from my cell. They left me in the straight jacket that time.

The same doctor said, "I apologize for your first visit here, but we tell everybody that to see how they react! If they respond, we know there's hope. Pete, there's a lot of hope for you."

They showed me ink blotches, and I was supposed to tell them what they meant. I decided psychiatrists were loony, too. For seventeen days they had me on a drug that made me feel like a zombie. Later they put a pill in my mouth, and I'd go into the bathroom and spit it out. For three days I did that, so I felt like bouncing off the wall.

I calmed myself down, but then an aide came up to me and said, "Pete, I'll deny ever saying this, but they have you scheduled for shock treatments. I've had to look over all your records, and the only thing wrong with you is you've had one heck of a pile of bad luck. I'm going to arrange for you to have a three-hour pass to walk around. I never want to see you again."

That place was history! People panicked when I got home. Everyone was on pins and needles if I was around. I went back after ninety days, then two times a week for eleven months. After that, they said I didn't need to come back, which fractured me. Every time I'd been completely ripped; I was so full of drugs.

Everybody I ran with had drugs. We had them shipped from Vietnam, from buddies in New Mexico. I'd hand out the drugs and collect the money. I had everything I wanted, including a Harley and an endless supply of free drugs, because I short-changed everybody. If someone wanted a pound, I'd give them fifteen ounces. You can't live on the edge like that forever.

My mother had me talking to some ministers, and my mom was a baby Christian at the time. For three days I didn't eat or sleep; all I did was drink booze and wax my motorcycle in the garage.

I was in the basement when Mom came and stood at the top of the steps, "Pete, your problem is between you and God. I'm not leaving here until you talk to a minister."

"Get out of here and get off my back!," I yelled.

"I'm not leaving till you talk to a minister."

A light bulb went on. *I'll get even with God. I'll beat one of His chosen people — I'll beat His minister to death with my bare fists.* I said, "Call him on the phone, Mom." There was hope for me to get even with God!

The next day I was to go to the appointment at eight o'clock. I'd been eating black beauties all day long, smoking pot, and taking codeine. Every ninety days the government sent me a new supply of Tylenol with codeine because I was on disability. I took it all in thirty days. My body didn't know if it was up or down. I'd walked away from disasters and wrecks, and I told God, "All you want me to do is suffer. You won't kill me!" I wanted to hurt Him because I was hurting. This night was my night to get even.

My plan was to go at 8:30—late for the meeting. When I pounded on that door, I was certain that Rev. Jim Erb would come and say, "Pete Wasko, you're late."

The word "late" would be my cue to beat him to death. When he answered the door, my fists were clenched and ready. He said, "You must be Pete Wasko. Come in, you are right on time." No plan B—he didn't mention the word "late."

Like a little puppy, I followed Jim inside. We went into the kitchen where he used child psychology on me. "Your mother called and set this up, but you know how mothers are. She told me a little bit about you, but why don't you tell me yourself?"

I spilled my guts, and then that man who I intended to kill led me to the Lord. He shared about the forgiving grace of Jesus, and I prayed the sinner's prayer. I had a lot to repent of; but when I left Jim Erb's house that night, I felt perfectly clean!

Monday I was back on drugs. Jim had told me, "One of the things you have to do as a Christian, Pete, is to renew your mind. You can't hang around the friends you had before because this is something new. Bad company corrupts your morals, so you need to get around other Christians and be an imitator of Christ."

I decided to go to "The Barn," a place on the Watson farm where young people gathered every Thursday night. When I went in, I saw people had their hands in the air, praising the Lord. The pain in my back was unbearable as I sat down on the floor. Part of the reason I'd taken so many drugs was because I hurt so much.

At the end of the service, the speaker asked for prayer requests. I challenged God, "If you are the God you claim to be, then heal my back." I stood up.

People came over and laid hands on me. It felt like the hands of LOVE on my back. The pain disappeared! It has never come back! When I walked out, the power of the Living Lord was all over me.

Yet Monday I was right back in my mud hole. The following Thursday Rev. Dick Burns was the guest speaker at "The Barn." He prayed about our making a mess out of our lives by the decisions we make. He said, "If you don't know where you're going when you leave here tonight, I'd like to pray with you." Before I left for the prayer meeting that night, I had told my wife, "It's over and when the meeting is done I'm leaving." She asked, "Where are you going?" I said, "I don't know. It doesn't matter anyway." I knew Rev. Burns was referring to heaven or hell, so I shot up front where he laid his hands on my head. It felt as though a bolt of lightning went through me, and I was on fire for God. I began speaking in tongues.

The Lord Jesus spared me from drugs, the war, myself, but I still had to have my mind renewed. Seventeen years after Vietnam I found that if the temperature was right, or I was walking down a country road, the circumstances could trigger a flashback; and I had to relive the horrors of the war all over again. Nightmares, waking up screaming, not able to go to sleep—there I was, a born-again Christian, going through all this horror all over again!

During a fasting and praying time, the Lord reminded me of David. Didn't I think that David had any flashbacks about the battles he'd been in?

"No, Lord, David was only doing what he was supposed to do."

"Pete, you were just doing what you were told."

I thought that if it didn't bother the Lord, it shouldn't bother me.

For a while the flashbacks stopped, then they resumed. One day I was looking out the window, and I felt the presence of God. It was as though I was inside my own mind and God was sitting on the throne. Jesus Christ and I were standing next to God. Satan kept running up to Jesus and saying, "He did this—He did that—He's no good." "He" meant me!

Jesus answered his adversary, "I shed my blood for him, so that he doesn't have to go through this anymore."

This was all in my head, and my ears were like the doors to God's court room. *"Now listen,"* God said, *"there is no condemnation for those who are in Christ Jesus. Here's how to discern your thoughts and words: would Jesus Christ do or say what your mouth and mind are thinking and saying?"*

That made me think about the adverse things I say. Are they from God? No! Would He give me flashbacks? No! If they aren't from God—who are they from? Satan was still trying to destroy my mind and actions.

I learned then to send them out of my mind. Satan can't give me flashbacks anymore. Another day I asked the Lord, "Why would You forgive the horrible things I did in Vietnam?"

His answer came as clear as a bell, "Because I love you."

Jesus doesn't just love and bless Pete Wasko. He left the ninety and nine to find the little lost sheep. Jesus, King of Kings, Lord of Lords, wants YOU to be well and free from the sins of yesterday. All you have to do is to tell Him you're sorry and need His forgiveness. He loved you enough to die for you. Now He wants you to live the abundant life for Him.

* * * * *

Dr. Pete Wasko and his family currently reside in western Pennsylvania. He has had his dreams fulfilled beyond his greatest imagination by completing training in Atlanta, GA, and is now a licensed chiropractor (D.C.) and has his offices at 210 W. Neshannock Ave., New Wilmington, PA 16142.

Freed from Bondage

Rocco Morelli

"Little Chicago," the nickname that my hometown of New Kensington, PA, had because of its Mob connections, wasn't a misnomer. At one point in time, my birthplace was mentioned in the Guiness Book of Records for having more bars per block than any other city. Frank Sinatra and many Mafia bosses were frequent visitors there. My Mob connection came from my great grandfather who was a famous Don from Sicily who lived a double standard. He was the only one allowed to play the organ in his private chapel, but he saw nothing wrong in living a corrupt political life. Money, power, and prestige were his even though he never seemed to care how he got them.

My grandfather, the Don's son, brought some of his friends to America, partially to escape from the influence of the Mob and his powerful father. Yet Grandpa's efforts were in vain, for several Mafia families accompanied him to Ellis Island and then on to New Kensington where my dad was born.

My father broke the great Italian tradition by marrying a sweet Russian-Ukrainian girl. He could have been ousted from the clan because of this marriage, but instead other clan members called him "Dago Red." After all, Pop bore the infamous Morelli name.

Dad was the typical Italian churchgoer who paid lip service on Sunday to his Maker. I found out that Mom and her prayer partner gave their hearts to Christ at a young age at a Tent Revival Meeting, and started attending healing services at Kathryn Kuhlman's. My mother's prayer partner later became a choice member of Kathryn Kuhlman's.

My mom backslid with her religion when she met my dad. She went from Russian-Orthodox to Roman Catholicism. She recommitted her life to Christ when I suffered a breakdown. My dad, and my mom's sister Olga, gave their hearts to Christ for the first time at a church service they attended to pray for me. This service was at an Open Door Bible Church where an Evangelist was conducting a Revival Service near the hospital where I was in Indiana.

The Mafia curse was on me. As my parents' only child, Mom and Dad wanted the best for me, but not as much as I did. Power-hungry, I started my own band. At age 15 we were out playing in night clubs. Wine, women, and song consumed my thoughts and ambitions. Like "Old Blue Eyes," I wanted it "My Way."

During the years that followed, I kept my feet in both worlds —the legitimate and illegitimate — so much so that even though I was involved in Mob activities — I became a cop at the age of 19.

The lure of the underworld possessed me. I'd play cop during the day and go to the dives and be a robber at night. I learned about the "Pizza Connection" — that some pizza houses served as fronts across the country for narcotic connections. I became a pusher and eventually messed up my mind by mixing drugs and alcohol.

All through this time, Mom never ceased to pray for her errant son. Dad even bargained with God when I became hospitalized with mental problems. Thank God for my parents! I got better and was released from the mental hospital.

But I hadn't learned my lesson. Still power-hungry, I was an Italian who wanted more and more money — more and more of everything. I got married and had a beautiful baby girl named Racquel.

As was Mob tradition, I kept a mistress on the side. You'd have thought that all the wonderful things I had would have satisfied me, but there was never enough to keep Rocco Morelli content. I was looking for that something that would fill the emptiness I felt inside.

With my best friend, I became more involved in drug connections. Then one Sunday suddenly the house was filled with Swat Team uniforms. I had a concealed gun on me so I tossed it aside, fearing they would kill me if they found I was armed. "Look," I said, "I have nothing on me."

After they took me to jail, I realized they wanted me for a "Wise Guy" just like the TV movie used to show. The cops wanted me to squeal on the Mob — my friends! For six weeks I had them going on a merry-go-round. The Mob got through to me to let me know that a contract was put out on the guy who squealed. Who was the rat? — Tony, my "best friend!" Who was to fulfill the contract? ME!!

Because of refusing to cooperate with the police and be an informer, I was going to have to go through a trial. While out on bail, I went to my doctor friend, Frank Iozzi. For years he'd patched me up. Whenever I got in scrapes I'd go to him and he'd witness to me about Christ. I'd half-listen because I thought so much of him, but I was sure that his Christian "stuff" wasn't going to do anything for me. Besides, regardless of the fact that I was about to go to jail, I was ROCCO MORELLI, and I could take care of myself!

When Frank offered me free tickets to go to a dinner, I accepted them. I took Tony with me for the boys in the Mafia always said, "Keep your enemies closer than a brother."

While waiting to go into the dinner, I looked around and saw everyone smiling and hugging each other. I wondered, *"Did they all hit the lottery?"* I'd never seen such a bunch of happy people!

We all sat down with my "best friend" right beside me. Everyone stood up and sang and declared "Praise the Lord!" What a bunch of characters! When I looked at Tony, I realized the whole scene was making him uncomfortable. Not me! I was befuddled. What was going on?

I'd planned to do away with my former buddy to get revenge and mob status, but after the speaker started, I got so caught up in what he was saying that I forgot Tony was even there. The guy up front said his name was Steve Totin. As he related his life story and how he'd had doubts about Christianity all of his life, I thought, *He's no different than I am.* Steve was somebody I could relate to. When he spoke about how he came to Christ, it seemed so simple.

Tony left. I didn't follow him. It was as if I was glued to my seat. Could Jesus really change my life? Could anyone really fill the empty spot I had inside? As Steve Totin kept on speaking, I thought he was talking directly to me.

When the line formed for prayer, I joined the others. There I was, about to go to prison for numerous bad crimes, and I stood waiting in a prayer line! It was as if an unseen magnet was drawing me.

When my turn for prayer came, I found myself asking Jesus to forgive me and come into my heart as Steve directed. Jesus came. Rocco Morelli, tough mobster, never felt more humble than I did at that moment.

I knew Jesus answered my prayer. Steve laid hands on me, and I went down on the floor. Such a peace came over me. Such joy! I was headed for prison, but I felt as though I'd been released from the power-hungry curse that had plagued me all of my life.

Steve Totin's wife claimed she had a prophecy, "You and Steve are going to work in prison together."

To this her husband objected, "He's going to jail. I'm not!"

I left that place a new creation. Yet I did have to pay a

price for my past crimes just as the scripture says. *"What you sow, you also reap."*

My sentence could be up to twenty years, but after Dr. Iozzi and others appeared as character witnesses on my behalf, the judge reduced the sentence to two years. That proved that my mom was praying extra hard, but I was also aware that her years of praying had been the most important fruit she ever wanted. Her errant son had come to the Lord!

In prison I witnessed to many convicts. Because I was one of them, my cell-mates were more willing to listen. Many, even the most hard core criminals, softened when they were told the Bible's most personal message, "Jesus loves you."

Mrs. Totin's prophetic words came true. Steve was affiliated with Cornerstone Television out of Wall, PA, and he invited me to be the first inmate to ever appear on TV to give my testimony. Collect phone calls began coming in from prisoners across the country. Knowing that the prisoners needed to communicate, Russ and Norma Bixler and staff decided to minister to them at CTV's expense. The prison ministry was born!

My wife had been upset about my arrest and conviction and the total change in our life. Even my professing that I'd make Jesus Lord of my life seemed alien to her. She finally brought our baby along to visit, but after that something out of my control took place. The woman I'd had an adulterous affair with came by my wife's office to inquire about me. What recourse do you have when your wife is confronted by your former mistress? None — especially when you're behind bars! I tried and tried to call her and convince her that I'd honestly changed, but my pleas for her not to get a divorce fell on deaf ears.

Heartbroken, I went to Jesus for consolation. Through my tears, I read scripture after scripture telling of God's promises. Even through that dark period of despair, I did not quit witnessing about the Lord and His love. Steve and

I continued the prison ministry.

Prison garb and jail bars became such a part of my existence that I could scarcely believe it when the parole board decided to let me go after only eighteen months of my two year sentence. Mom and Dad had visited me at every opportunity during my imprisonment, so I knew how hurt they had been. Seeing their grim faces made me pray earnestly that I would never be the reason for them to anguish any more.

Mom and Dad were waiting to take me home to be with them — welcoming me with open arms. My heart's desire was to have a ministry for prisoners not only for inmates, but for men who had been incarcerated and needed some Godly direction to help keep them from being repeat offenders — to establish and maintain an "After Care Center." Few of them were as fortunate as I was. Most of the men I talked with in jail came from dysfunctional families and had a very poor upbringing. They needed a place to be able to rehabilitate themselves to learn to make a living and cope with society again.

The next few years I went through many trials, but the Holy Spirit never let me falter and fall into such sin again. Every time the lure of the casinos and the fast life of the Mafia tempted me in any way, I'd say, "In the name of Jesus — get thee behind me, Satan!"

Yet life was not easy. I made some mistakes - not Mafia-type errors — but some. I yearned for security and a loving spouse; but for a long period of time, I could not seem to learn what direction to head to do the work that I felt God wanted for me. I needed a help-mate.

At a Full Gospel banquet one night, I saw this blonde young woman, and I felt the Holy Spirit nudging me, assuring me that she was "the one."

During the months that ensued Chris and I bonded with the Love of the Lord. Christine told me that she had prayed for a mate that she could minister with, one who would pray with her and share her love for Jesus.

We both had the inner assurance that the Lord wanted us to be together, so we pledged our wedding vows at the Salvation Army Church in New Kensington where I held weekly Revival Services over the Christmas holidays that year.

Since that time we have moved to a piece of land in Brookville, PA, where our intent is to eventually build the center that I feel the Lord wants us to create to help prisoners readjust to civilian life. "I was in prison and you visited me" — yes, I did that and I will continue to go to jails to witness about the love of Jesus; but more than that, Chris and I pray that we can minister to them at our God-oriented "After Care Center" soon.

As I reflect on years past when I was in the Mob and could have easily been killed, I realize that the Lord has always had His hand on me, and His angels must have been assigned to protect me because He has a job for me to do. My prayers often ask Him for guidance and direction to do it well.

* * * * *

World Reach is an interdenominational, non-profit Christian organization that ministers the good news of Jesus Christ to prisoners around the world. Our church affiliation is underneath the covering and leadership of Gospel Assemblies International. We are network members of C.O.P.E. (Coalition of Prison Evangelists) and Bridge Builders which is a Christ-centered, 12-step recovery ministry and program. We are focused on reaching those with life-controlling problems such as drug and alcohol addictions, at-risk kids, and their families. Our goal is to teach discipline and raise up Godly individuals for the army of Christ. A foundation has been created to raise necessary funds to provide spiritual, physical, emotional, and financial help to those who are poor, hungry, and homeless; to rehabilitate ex-offenders and prisoners; reintegrate families — both socially and spiritually — by ministering to the whole person through Complete Care Programs.

For more information about our ministry programs or to invite us to share the Word, our testimonies, and visions, please contact our ministry at:

World Reach
HC6 Box 117C
Brookville, PA 15825
814-328-5021
Fax: 814-328-5053
e-mail: reachout@penn.com

Free Indeed!

Ann Thomas

"I abhor the bugs that crawl over my skin! I loathe these horrid worms that wriggle out of my flesh!" I grappled for an instrument. Anything sharp would do. I settled for a needle. I picked. I dug. I scraped at the evil creatures; still they persisted!

How was I to know that drugs had distorted my mind and created these horrid hallucinations? The spirit of death was following me and trying to kill me. I could have life, but I didn't know that in John 10:10 Jesus said, *"The thief cometh not, but for to steal, and to kill, and to destroy: I am come that they might have life, and that they might have it more abundantly."*

As a teenager, I hated farming! I hoed corn. I hoed and picked cotton. One day when I was working in the fields, a good-looking young man drove by in a flatbed truck loaded with bales of cotton. I hadn't met him, but I knew he was Howard Thomas, and his father owned the nearby cotton gin.

I leaned on my hoe and spoke what turned out to be prophetic. I said, "I'm going to marry that boy and be a doctor's wife, not a farmer's wife."

Although Father was a leader in the church and Mother, a Sunday School teacher, there was tension and strife in our home. I knew there was more to the Christian life, but

I didn't know what it was or where to find it.

Howard and I began dating. When we were married, we read the Bible and were under conviction; but we didn't know what to do about it.

After two years of marriage, when Jimmy was about eight months old, Howard started college at Memphis State University. After graduation, he went to the University of Tennessee Medical School in Memphis. At the parties, everyone was drinking and smoking. I knew it was wrong, but I wanted to fit in — so I started drinking and smoking, too.

Howard interned in Atlanta then opened his medical practice in Henderson, Tennessee. We began to make a lot of money. I went to bridge parties and tried to be a good doctor's wife. We did a lot of things at parties that I knew were wrong. I was miserable!

Finally, I turned to Howard. "I can't stand living like this any longer. Please give me a shot of something to help me cope."

I didn't know it, but he was already on drugs. My first shot made me feel great. I was floating. The next night, I wanted another one — and the next night, another. Drugs were an aid, then a crutch, but quickly they became a dependency. Before long, I was "main lining." Drugs were destroying my life.

After Joseph was born, we moved to Miami, Arizona. I was so heavily into drugs that I don't remember the move. I had a maid to do the housework and to watch the children, so I went out and did things. I don't know where I went or what I did.

Eventually, I was crazed. I ripped curtains down from the windows. I thought worms and bugs were coming out of my skin. I could literally see them coming out of my body. I was filled with demons.

Howard was high on drugs all the time, too. He wrecked the car. We were sued. Both high, we went to court. Even the judge didn't recognize that we were on drugs. Where were we to get help?

We returned to Acton, Tennessee. Satan did his evil number on me. He told me I was no good as a mother or as a wife. In an effort to commit suicide, I overdosed. Howard found me in a catatonic state and took me to a psychiatric hospital in Memphis. It took twenty-one shock treatments to bring me to where I could function again, but everything had been blocked out. I didn't remember I had a husband or three children. I remained at the institution for about three months. Gradually my memory returned.

After I was released, I began working in the office with Howard. My doctor had prescribed medication; thus I got right back on drugs. Problems gradually escalated. Howard and I got to where we would take as high as 30 shots and 50 pills a day. In about eight months, I was so filled with demons — it was horrid!

My beloved grandfather visited. I was so drugged, I told him I didn't have time for him. He just looked at me. Two weeks later, he died. My parents were so ashamed of what I'd become and embarrassed by my actions that they would not let me attend the funeral. I was crushed; still, I didn't change.

Howard moved his practice to Selmer, Tennessee. Things got even worse. Jimmy, who was now eleven, began to pray. After the third night, an angel appeared to him. His bedroom lit up like a ball of fire. The angel said, "My son, your mommy and daddy will be saved and you will have a happy life."

Concerned about what I was becoming, Mother tried to get me out of the house. Howard would not let me go. He had guns, and he'd threatened me. He's sweet now. Then, he was demon possessed.

Mama had told the maid to let her know if I called out for her. I cried for her when I was in bed. I weighed only eighty pounds and was covered with sores. Because of the worms I thought were in my flesh, I had dug at myself with anything sharp I could get hold of. This, created scars on my body.

Mama came. They rushed me to the same hospital. The doctor said he didn't think he could save me this time.

Unbeknown to me, time proceeded. Mama had been with me in the hospital. On her way home, 120 miles away in Memphis, she saw a group of ladies entering a Pentecostal church. She stopped and ask them to pray for me because I was on drugs and was dying. They began to pray in the Spirit. My mother would not have been caught dead in that Pentecostal church, but we do a lot of things when we're desperate. Since, I've learned, *"The true worshiper will worship me in spirit and in truth."* John 4:23.

I didn't know Mama was praying. I blinked, and gray walls came into focus. I realized I was in a hospital. I was dying! Suddenly I felt the presence of the Holy Spirit.

I'm not saved! "God, I've made a mess of my life!"

He began revealing himself to me, and I rebuked the evil spirits. "I hate these drugs. I don't want you. I will not let you stay in my body. Leave, in the name of Jesus." They left.

After rebuking the demons, I fell into a deep sleep. When I woke, my mind was clear. It was the first time in ages. A miracle had taken place. I didn't know why or understand, but I no longer wanted to take drugs, and I knew that I wouldn't.

I left the hospital, stayed with Mama for a week, then went home to Selmer. Howard was sitting on the sofa. He looked up. "Do you want a shot?"

"No! And don't ever ask me again!"

I wondered how I had resisted. Something good had happened to me. I didn't know what.

One day a narcotics agent called. "Your husband is having a problem with drugs, isn't he?"

"Yes."

"We're coming by to get him."

"He needs to be taken to where he can get help."

"That's what we intend to do."

"You'd better make sure Howard is sleeping when you

come for him, or he'll kill you, and he'll kill me!"

The agents came when Howard was sound asleep and took him to Murfreesboro, Tennessee. This was the second time for him.

He escaped. The FBI came to me. I went home. Howard had been there and had taken his doctor's bag. He left a note telling the boys that he loved them but left no message for me.

A few days later, Howard phoned and asked me to join him in Morenci, Arizona. I didn't feel that I could make a living to support myself and three little boys, so I agreed to go. My father took me — against his will and better judgment, for Howard was still on drugs.

I began to meet new people and started to bowl. I won the city tournament. What a victory for me! At last I was a winner at something. I went to the international tournament in Phoenix with a carload of ladies. One of them, a nurse at the hospital, turned to me. "Something is going to happen. Your husband is falling asleep during surgery, and I'm having to kick him to keep him awake. And, did you know that he is about to get married?"

"No!" This threw me for a loop! I knew my husband was on drugs and that he drove aimlessly around at night, but I didn't expect this! I remembered that one of the other doctors had made comments, but I hadn't caught on. I realized I'd better do something, not only for my sake, but for Howard's.

My bowling buddies were used to the ways of the world. They wanted to stop at a bar. I didn't want to because I'd recently come off drugs and I didn't want to drink. I said, "I'm going to make a phone call." I intended to hire a detective to follow Howard and find out what was going on. I went into a phone booth. There was a tract with the bold words, *"If Jesus Came to Your House."* I read it and knew if Jesus came to mine, he'd find a mess. I believed God was letting me know in His own sweet, gentle way that He was around and still cared for us.

Later I discovered that the detective couldn't help me because it was out of his jurisdiction. I went home defeated, confused, and afraid. I didn't know that, *"...faith is the substance of things hoped for, the evidence of things not seen."* Hebrews 11:1.

Howard got lost in the desert. I told the truth about his being on drugs. He was fired. After he was found, he spent a month with his parents. We then moved to Saltillo, Tennessee, where they needed a clinic. I was off of drugs, but I was still trying to get my act together. I was working with Howard. He was so doped up that a lot of times I had to sew people up. I delivered babies because he couldn't stay awake. It was terrible, but the people loved him anyway.

The situation worsened. I started going to parties. I was headed for trouble. God spoke to me, and I knew it was for the last time. He said, *"This is it, Ann."*

I didn't know what to do spiritually. My parents were now committed Christians, so I called Mama. "I'm getting a divorce and coming home."

I got a job and was doing pretty well. Then, one day Howard came! He said he'd gotten saved. He didn't make a big issue about it; he doesn't make big issues. He wanted me to come back. I refused.

God gave him a Scripture verse. *"Seek ye first the kingdom of God, and his righteousness, and all these things will be added unto you."* Matthew 6:33.

Three weeks later Howard returned. The devil had tried to get him back, but determined, Howard had stood his ground. I thank God he did. He was scheduled to give his testimony in a little Methodist church, and he wanted me to go with him.

Mama didn't want me to go, but I went. I had stopped drinking and drugs, too, and I thought I was as good as Howard. I sat at the back of the church; Howard went forward and began talking about Jesus. He took the Bible and held it up. I felt lost. I thought, *Well, you have to get lost to get found.*

Howard kept holding the Bible up and talking. I thought, *Lord this is what I want*. When Howard finished talking, I ran to the altar and fell on my face. "God! I mean business!"

In a vision, I saw my Lord and the blood that flowed from his wounds. God showed me that my body was the temple of the Holy Spirit, so I knew before I read in the Word, *"Know ye not that your body is the temple of the Holy Ghost which is in you, which ye have of God, and ye are not your own?"* I Corinthians 6:19.

I cried out for God's forgiveness and was washed clean by the blood of the Lamb. I had a deep love for my husband that I had never had. I decided to go back to him.

Mama was afraid I was making another mistake. I explained that the Lord Jesus had entered my heart and had forgiven me for everything wrong I had done. Howard, too, had been cleansed. I told her about my vision and how the Holy Spirit had done work in my life. "Mama, Howard, and I are going to make it with Jesus."

In the days that followed, a passage from Psalm 139 became dear to me. *"You knit me together in my mother's womb. I praise you because I am fearfully and wonderfully made. Your works are wonderful; I know that full well...All the days ordained for me were written in your book before one of them came to be."* God has a definite plan and purpose for our lives.

Howard and I were thankful for our new beginning. We started blessing everything we ate, everywhere we went, everything we did. Satan kept reminding me of the horrid things I'd done. I would say, "Jesus, Jesus, Jesus." The devil would flee, for he hates the name of Jesus.

I hated smoking and longed to quit. Howard and I prayed together; then we joined about thirty-five people and started praying. That night I received deliverance from smoking. I threw my cigarettes away and never smoked another one.

We built a new house and dedicated it to God. I knew that when the Lord sets you free, you are free indeed; however, I was afraid to speak in front of people. The ladies in the church said I needed Holy Spirit power in my life to enable me to witness.

During revival, I received the Baptism of the Holy Spirit and prayed in the Spirit for two hours. I'd been drunk on alcohol, but now I was drunk with the Spirit. I was having a glory hallelujah time. I had wondered why people said, "Thank you, Jesus" all the time. I found out! My praise flowed like a river, and the glory of God has been flowing ever since. He is Creator and Sustainer. Praise the name of the Lord!

Since Howard and I gave our lives to Christ, we have been traveling to witness about the glory of the Lord. He rescues. He forgives. He cleanses. He empowers with His Holy Spirit. *"He who the Son has set free is free indeed."* Hallelujah!

Story as told to: Barbara Michel

* * * * *

Dr. Howard and Ann Thomas are located in Savannah, TN, and can be reached there or by calling Son-Rise Publications at 1-800-358-0777.

Dr. Howard Thomas

The Corporate Junky

Jerry Wilson

"Jeffrey, you need to straighten up and be like your Uncle Jerome. Make something of yourself like he did!" Those were my sister's words to our nephew later in life, but she always thought I was something special. Even when we were young and I was the baby, the whole family catered to me, especially Gladys.

When I grew up, I hoped to follow in my brother Freddie's footsteps and become a basketball star. Gladys helped me cope when Freddie fell victim to the devastating effects of leukemia. Our hearts were shattered when the whole family stood helplessly by as he got weaker and weaker. Then he died. My idol was gone. My ambition to be like him kept me pursuing a basketball career, and I did make a name for myself as a sports star both in high school and college.

During my years at Cheyney State University, I fell in love and married a vibrant cheerleader. We both thought the world was our oyster, and we were creating priceless pearls when we had two adorable little boys. After I left college, I went to work at US Steel as a lab technician. Few Blacks had such positions, and I was quite noticeable because it was difficult to get my wild hairdo under my hard hat when I had to go out on a site.

At the age of 29 I wanted to build a new career in sales

because I loved people, and interacting with them was always a joy and a challenge. One fear tore at my soul in that year of 1969. Would my skin color hinder me from fulfilling my ambitions in the corporate world? One encounter helped relieve my mind.

My wife and I had purchased a new car. The family was traveling to see her father who was ill when that Volkswagen broke down. I must have made quite a scene as a very angry 29-year-old Black man with a wild Afro tinkering under the hood of the broken-down vehicle. I finally noticed a distinguished looking, white man in a navy pin-striped suit standing by watching me.

"I'd like to help," he said. "I have a used-car dealership. We need to get you another car." This stranger took me in his Cadillac and offered me my choice of seven used cars to continue on my way. He said he'd see to it that my VW would be fixed.

I couldn't conceive of a white man being my Good Samaritan. "We can't get your vehicle back right away. It might take us a few days," I told our benefactor as I explained the situation with my sick father-in-law.

The stranger gave me my choice of vehicles, then handed me the keys to a station wagon saying, "Take as long as you need".

After thanking him, we continued on our journey. Four days later I returned. He refused my offer to pay him and then invited me to his house. There he offered words of encouragement, "I see great potential in you. If only my own son had your dreams and aspirations. You can go far if you'll get that chip off your shoulder White men aren't all bad. I think you ought to apply for a sales job in either U.S. Steel or Xerox. Please feel free to use my name."

With that remarkable shove, I went to U.S. Steel and found the name "Phil Shoop" did open doors! My interviewer seemed very interested, but he finally declared, "Jerry, I see your potential, but I don't think U.S. Steel is ready for you yet."

I knew what he was saying. They weren't prepared to hire a Black man at that time. When I left him I had a bitter feeling of rejection and dejection, but decided to send resumes to IBM and other major corporations anyway. To my surprise, all of them made me offers for employment. Xerox became my target because of its tremendous training program. They hired me!

Thrilled that they were willing to risk taking me on, I did an outstanding job for them. I kept going a little higher on the corporate ladder all the time. One day I delivered a machine to a customer, installed it, then reached out to shake hands with the store owner. I received a limp, reluctant, two-finger handshake in return.

Later my immediate supervisor phoned and said, "Jerry, your customer called and said he didn't want the machine if you were the one who was to service it. I'm going to call Mike and discuss this with him."

Mike Wood was my big boss. After hearing the problem, he phoned the customer and said, "Jerry Wilson is the finest we have. If you don't want him to service your account, we'll be glad to pull it."

He did! That very white-skinned Wood did that for me! After that I'd shed my red blood for Mike and Xerox.. Up, up and away I went, but I began compromising the strict religious upbringing I'd had at home by smoking and drinking with clients. While I was under my mother and father's roof, I'd gone to church with them, but I left my Christian heritage behind when I moved out at age seventeen.

My social drinking, my smoking, my late hours with clients took their toll. Friction built up between my wife and me. Then a friend introduced me to marijuana, saying, "Jerry it'll make you feel so relaxed." He was right. Smoking pot made me feel less stressed. But then, one Thursday night while working for Xerox in Atlanta, I was convinced by friends, who were smoking and snorting coke, to try it. Cocaine exhilarated me!

And so, I became a corporate junky. Instead of my newly-found high keeping me from making sales, I began to break all records. Records at home became broken too. My wife and I were in a continuous battle about what I was doing with my life. In 1975 we had a major battle and we separated. A promotion down south for Xerox came then, and I made my mark there as the "Billy Dee of Atlanta" with my sport cars and fancy clothes and my zest for women. Yet my father and mother never seemed to notice my drug and alcohol involvement and wondered what was wrong with my spouse. Gladys never failed to see me as her knight in shining armor.

Suddenly the rest of my world began falling apart. My older brother had three sons. John had a drinking habit, and he'd been beaten up out on the streets. He contracted pneumonia. As I waited for response to a 911 call for an ambulance, he died in my arms pleading, "Jerry, look out for my three sons." I was a poor one to put in charge of his offspring. Self-obsessed, I wasn't even doing well with my own boys.

Xerox transferred me to Philadelphia where they gave me the awesome responsibility of heading up the Navy and defense market. On December 8, 1980, I was out doing my Saturday night thing with drugs and drinking which lasted until 4 in the morning. Traveling down four-lane Lincoln Drive, a drunk crossed the center line — wham! He hit me head-on!

Not wearing a seat belt, I managed to grab my stash of drugs from my sock where I kept it hidden and tossed it away before I passed out. The ambulance came and rushed me to the hospital where they put my neck in a brace. An uncaring, rough nurse tried to scrape the windshield glass from my face. Limping and bruised, I went home.

I was staying with Mama at the time because I needed a home and she needed care. Her kidneys were failing and she had to be on dialysis. When my mother was coming down the steps after getting ready for church, she looked at me in disgust as I limped in the door. "Will you never learn?

You should go with me to church, but look at you! I told you that someday you're supposed to be a preacher!" Her barrage of accusing words threw me off guard. I just wanted my Mama to take me in her arms and console me, but all she did was chastise me and say that I should be a PREACHER!

The next day I went to my lawyer and to the doctor who sent me to the hospital to be in traction for two weeks. While I was there, with my neck being stretched, my wife's lawyer phoned and said, "Your divorce is final."

My world seemed to be falling apart. In January of 1981 my dear, close aunt died. In July Mama died. Gladys tried to console me through my domino-effect tragedies. My own consolation came through cocaine. For seventeen months I nursed my physical and mental anguish with coke, bought with insurance and disability money.

When my condition improved, I moved from Philadelphia, which thrilled me because of having built up a reputation of being a "hot shot" there. My career with Xerox kept building, but somehow the whole scene of fast living didn't appeal the same after awhile.

Back in Philadelphia while staying at my sister's house, I spent time with my nephew Jeffrey and snorted cocaine secretly with him. Gladys didn't know my vices then. She was still trying to raise our nephew who was in rebellion. He was one of the three sons I'd promised my brother John I'd help raise!

As soon as I left that day, my sister started on my nephew once again. "Jeffery, you need to straighten up your life! Look at your Uncle Jerome. He's such a success! You love him; why don't you want to be like him?"

Tired of the facade, he screamed back, "You want me to be like HIM? He's nothin' but a coke-head himself! How do I know? 'Cause I've done it with him."

His retort floored Gladys. My sister didn't know! I'd managed to hide my addiction from her for years.

Gladys, sickened at heart, began to pray for me, her

errant brother. She fasted for three days while she asked the Lord to do a five-fold miracle. To have me:
1. Come to Jesus and be born-again.
2. Thirst for the knowledge of God.
3. Be surrounded by born-again Christians.
4. Be baptized in the Holy Spirit with the evidence of my own prayer language.
5. Be delivered from the dreaded, deadly cocaine.

My sister never confronted me. Instead she prayed for all this behind my back. It worked! For some reason, unbeknownst to me, I began to feel convicted about what I was doing. One day I was snorting coke with friends when suddenly I felt as though I had been hit with a surge of electricity. I pushed my body from the table and startled myself and my long-time buddies by saying, "I don't think GOD would like what we're doing!"

They looked at me as though I'd suddenly grown two heads. I further amazed myself and them by walking away. What was wrong with me?

Stranger things began to happen. I felt an urging to get into the Bible, but first I had to dig one up. No one, least of all me, could understand why I would suddenly get an insatiable appetite for God's Word.

Yet, as I went through the scriptures, they somehow began to minister to me. A week later this "dope-head" corporate junky, Jerry Wilson, found himself down on his knees asking Jesus to forgive him from his sins and come into his heart. Mama didn't live to see it, but I knew she'd have danced in heaven if she knew her errant son had returned to the Father.

I rose from there a new creation! Later as I shared with Gladys what had taken place, she confessed that she had pleaded with the Lord to bring me to my senses. We both agreed that I should quit my secular job and go into Christian work.

Right after that experience in February of 1983, I met and married a wonderful Christian wife; and we have an eleven-year-old daughter. My sons and I are on good terms. I was asked to baptize my grandson, and my first wife was there. We have restored our relationship to friendship. All this mending of my family I know has come about because of Jesus. He has restored one thing at a time and is still in the restoration process.

He is also restoring my body which had been ravaged by drugs for years. I exercise, eat nutritious food, and find that Green Supreme™ with Barley Power™ has given me a new physical lift. The Bible is filled with references to barley, so I feel the Lord has brought it into my life to distribute; so much so that folks jokingly call me "The Barley Man!"

I have been *in the valley of the shadow of death and I fear no evil* for I have His rod and His staff to comfort me. He can do the same for you. King Jesus is in the restoration business! He has brought me joy!

Jesus said in James 5: 16— *"The effectual fervent prayer of a righteous man availeth much."* The Lord has proven His Word to be true. My sister's and mother's prayers have paid off in souls—I've gone from a corporate junky to a corporate evangelist. What's even more thrilling to me is Jeffery, the boy who had rebelled and been on drugs with me, has put Jesus into his heart and is now on fire for the Living Lord!

* * * * *

Jerry Wilson can be contacted for speaking engagements at 4241 Ridgetop Drive, Ellenwood, GA 30294. He not only evangelizes to spread the news of good health and spiritual well-being, but he is involved in promoting a sports invention—"Baseball Buddy." His phone number is 404-241-5704.

Hurt, Hope and Healing

Jeniece Learned

After having a lengthy relationship with my first boyfriend and experimenting with sex at the age of 16, I missed my period. Very scared and confused, I consulted with friends and told them of my dilemma. They knew of a well-known "clinic" in the area where I could find out why I had missed my period. As I look back and reflect, I see how much of a child I still was. The idea of a sequence of events that would eventually lead up to the murder of an innocent, unborn child was beyond me. And it was my child!

I believed the world's message, "It's just a blob of tissue." No sonograms or educational materials had ever been shown to me as part of sex education. I hadn't been told anything about the possible results of intimacy with a boy - not from my parents, not from the classroom, not from my peers.

An appointment at the clinic was just a phone call away. I was met by a sweet and bubbly receptionist who sent me to a restroom for a urine test. I sat in a waiting area, very nervous and unsure of what was happening. The receptionist declared, "Your test is positive." We then made an appointment for me to proceed to Step Number 2. I was unsettled about something at the time, but I didn't know what.

As I look back today, I realize that I didn't even know what "your test is positive" meant. I drove myself to the clinic and found that I was not alone. The room was full of young girls just like me. I was called into a back room to undress and climb upon a gurney. There were gurneys in front and gurneys behind me. Each had a girl with her legs propped up waiting for what, we did not know. It was an assembly line. All of us, I believe, were completely unaware that we were going to have our children taken from us. I don't remember hearing the machine that sucked my baby out from inside my womb, but I've been told it is 29 times more powerful than a home vacuum cleaner. All for $350. Abortion is about money. Not about a real or informed choice.

No one really talked to me except for a nurse who said, "We need to give you a Rho-Gam shot for future pregnancies." Although no one explained what is was, I am truly grateful for that shot. I could have miscarried my beautiful daughter due to opposing blood types. Can you see God's protection on my daughter and me?

The nurse also told me, "You will have some bleeding but just change your pad." All I could think was "GREAT - they've started my period!" How naive, uninformed and immature I was! Another nurse came up and offered me some juice without saying a word. How I wanted to get out of there just as fast as I could. It seemed I'd been there forever. I had to be experiencing someone else's life. The whole ordeal was like a dream, it didn't seem real to me. For most women after their abortion, the relief that it's over is very strong; but my experience would not be over for two more days.

Because of not wanting anyone to know, I'd driven myself to the abortuary (clinic), and so I had to drive myself home. Still unsure of what had really taken place, I got ready that afternoon and went off to my job at a fast-food restaurant. Hard stomach cramps and much blood frightened me. I asked to go home from work. Panic hit as the cramps increased, and I hemorrhaged blood clots which seemed to be the size of grapefruits. As the severity of the pain increased, so did my fear. This hemorrhaging continued for two days. I did not realize until later this was not normal bleeding after an abortion. I praise God for His intervention even though I had not known His love at that time.

In 1981 at the age of 20, the Lord came into my life. Unbeknownst to me at the time, when I asked Jesus into my heart and asked for forgiveness for my sin, I accepted forgiveness for my abortion. He is faithful and just to forgive ALL unrighteousness. The abortion had been against the Lord, my child, and myself.

While in college in 1985, I saw a video entitled, "The Silent Scream," by Dr. Nathonson. A pro-life organization was putting on a seminar when they showed the film. For the first time I witnessed a real, live, first-trimester abortion being done. My own experience of having a "positive test," all came back to me. The wall of denial I had so tried to keep up came crashing down. For the first time I viewed it as "murder"— murder of my own baby. I was horrified at this truth being revealed to me.

After seeing the film, I flew out of that chapel service, it was all so surreal. Outside I stood against a wall; I couldn't breathe. My pain was that intense. The wall I'd tried to keep up, God dashed away in a matter of moments. My life was changed dramatically. I received counseling through that crisis pregnancy center. As a result, I started counseling girls that came in with crisis pregnancies, telling them that Jesus forgives ALL our sins.

I was married in 1983 to a wonderful man. In 1986 when we had our first child, I lay nursing my new baby. For four days I stayed in that bed. Very depressed, I cried and prayed and asked God for forgiveness over and over again. The realization had hit me full-force that I had committed murder of my innocent child. It was truly unbearable. On the fourth day I felt God say to me, "I have your baby and you ARE forgiven. Now, get up!" Peace fell over me. Over the past twelve years God has worked in my life to heal wounds that still lingered. Healing is truly an on-going process, one that has been fruitful and rewarding for me. Joy can come through the love of the Lord in spite of our sins.

All the while, being afraid to tell my mother, I had kept the abortion a secret for many years. I didn't know what she might do to me. How could I explain to her that her daughter had a first-time experience with sex and wound up pregnant? How would she feel? I knew I deprived my mother of having a choice to save her grandchild and loving her own child. She carried me in her own womb, and how I wish now that I had confided in her. Several years ago I asked my mother's forgiveness. She and I had a very healing time in our relationship. Another area of my abortion experience was healed in an awesome way on that snowy winter day.

What about the other person in my abortion experience? It takes two to make a baby. So, five years ago I asked the father of my child for his forgiveness and apologized to him for not giving him a chance or a choice in the decision. He forgave me. I hadn't realized how badly I'd hurt him. Women and babies are NOT the only victims of abortion. A trip to an abortuary encompasses all those who are a part of your life. Big boys do cry and hurt from the consequences of abortion. Grandparents grieve and siblings wonder, "Why was I spared?"

"Abortion" is a word game with a meaning that has not changed in 25 years. Why are girls still receiving the same "non-education" of what really takes place in the womb? Why are little girls and even married women not being told the truth about what is growing inside them? They're not given all the choices of an unintended pregnancy. No one told me about the possibility of adoption and what a loving choice that is.

We all know the answers to these "Why?" questions. Abortion clinics stand to lose perhaps millions and millions of dollars each year if abortion becomes illegal. People will lose jobs, and companies will lose money. My heart cries out to the millions of women who are still suffering from the traumatic after-shock of abortion. It's now been more than a quarter of a century since Roe vs. Wade was argued in the Supreme Court, and the babies that have been lost add up to over 35 million.

If you or a loved one suffers from a past abortion, you can get the healing that you so badly need. God has given me a full and joyous life in spite of my wrong, hurtful, and sinful decisions. He can do the same for you. Accepting the responsibility for your actions and repenting is the first step to a life full of peace. It's up to you. After the hurt, there is hope, then may you find healing in Jesus.

I direct an organization called P.L.E.A. (Pro-Life Education Alliance, a volunteer organization). It is my prayer that as I share with teenagers in the schools about the benefits of abstinence, that some unintended pregnancies may be spared. P.L.E.A. offers the option of adoption to girls and women who are caught in unintended pregnancies, and we serve to take women that have had past abortions through the grieving process. Education is the key in understanding the issues of abortion and free sex that surmount our society. Choose to educate and empower yourself with truth. Help to make a difference in this world! Our prayer and our plea is that we can make a difference together because of our love for Jesus.

* * * * *

Jeniece can be contacted at P.L.E.A., PO Box 644 / 107 West Venango Street, Mercer, PA 16137—(724) 662-HOPE(4673). She can put you in contact with caring Christians in any part of the country for assistance with pro-life issues or past-abortion counseling.

Green Light Means "Go"

Joe Cooper

"Joe, please don't go!" My wife Ellie ran after the plane, pleading for me not to make my planned dive from the sky. Regardless of the windy weather, I'd made up my mind to jump during a benefit show for a children's charity.

No one else was so foolish that day, and I wound up wishing I'd heeded both my wife and the weatherman's advice. During the six weeks afterward when I had to nurse a broken leg, my wife never once put me down by saying, "I told you so." She just loved me.

Ellie and I still have a special thing going between us. My crush on her began in high school and continued via letter when we both went to separate colleges. After I decided to join the army and was with the 11th Airborne stationed at Fort Campbell, Kentucky, I got to jump out of great aircraft and began to enjoy hearing what a brave and tremendous fellow I was.

A red light gave us the signal to get ready to jump from out of one of those big military transports. When the green light came, you knew that you had no choice – jump or be court-martialed! After my first awesome trip of floating to earth suspended from a parachute, no one needed to worry about my ignoring the signal to "GO." That thrill was so awesome that I could hardly wait for the green light to tumble out the door.

My army stint brought me my second love – falling from a plane with a parachute gave me a thrill unequaled by anything I'd ever done. I talked Ellie into becoming Mrs. Joe Cooper a little earlier than we planned so we could both take advantage of a year in Germany courtesy of Uncle Sam.

When I left the army as a combat engineer, I planned to work in steel construction; so we went back home to Ohio close to where we went to high school in Louisville, and became partners in a construction firm in nearby Alliance. For several years I enjoyed working with big equipment.

Ellie and I were blessed with two boys, Mark and Dean. I continued my vent for sky diving for years until I came down out of the wild blue yonder one day, and there I took a serious look at my family's faces. Boredom! Had I been so selfish that I'd forced my obsession on them? The broken leg clinched the deal. I had too much time to meditate on what I was doing to my family. At that point Joe Cooper gave up being suspended from a chute after 948 jumps!

As far as my Christian upbringing—I'd been baptized in the Neshannock Presbyterian Church in New Wilmington, PA, and had gone to Sunday School and church all my life. At the age of 12 I went to confirmation classes where I was taught the books of the Bible, but I don't remember learning any of their contents then. When I joined the church and took communion for the first time, I must have had an initial experience with the Holy Spirit; for I felt something so special that I thought it was in the juice. I wanted to bottle it for future use!

I believed that Jesus was the King of Kings and Lord of Lords then, but He wasn't my Lord. People might say I was saved then, but I didn't know it. So, therefore, I don't think I could have been.

Both my wife and I thought we should raise our kids in the church, and I decided to teach Sunday School to teach senior high students. In fact, I had several valedictorians in the class. They asked intelligent questions, but I didn't have answers. During those years I watched TV and often said "yes" in my mind to Billy Graham's calls to come forward, but I never confessed Jesus vocally. Sometimes tears would course down my cheeks.

Ellie and I had begun to read the Bible until we got to the "begats' in Genesis. I found that my knowledge of the Scriptures was so pitiful that I decided to attend Rev. Humbard's summer Bible School on Makinaw Island up in Michigan. I took Ellie and the kids there, thinking it would provide us with a family vacation as we learned more about the Word of God. Fascinated with getting more knowledge about Jesus, I took Ellie and the boys to an evening service Rex was holding. Before the service I'd told my wife and kids that I intended to go forward if he held an altar call.

I listened to Rex Humbard preach that Jesus was the Son of God, and there was no other way to get right with the Lord, that by Christ's death on the cross we were forgiven and Jesus Christ took all our sins upon Himself.

After that Rex gave the expected invitation to come forward to accept Jesus as Lord and Savior. I sat there, feeling too embarassed to move. How could I let anyone think I wasn't a Christian! How could I make a fool out of myself by going up to the altar?

The second call came. Rex declared, "All of you who want to accept Jesus and want to be born again, you'll have to get out of your seats and come down front." The move of the Holy Spirit was so strong that I shut my eyes to get it out of my system.

When the third invitation was issued, I closed my eyes once more. I saw two lights – red and green. From my military experience I knew that I could suffer severe repercussions if I didn't respond to the lights: red to get ready, green to go.

I went. I bailed out for Jesus! To my surprise I found myself gooey-eyed, then tears flooded my cheeks. No one can explain the joy, the peace, the thrill I had unless they have also given their hearts to Him. I had found another love! I stood there and said to Jesus, "I'm sorry. I accept You as my Lord and Savior .'

Life has never been the same. I was born again and I KNEW I was born again. Whatever happened in the past didn't matter. *"Behold, I make all things new."* I KNEW that I KNEW—no one had to tell me. Jesus had crossed my path and I had accepted Him into my heart.

My next surprise came when I realized my sons were both beside me – one on each side. *Oh Lord, how great can one moment be – not only to accept You into my heart, but to have Mark and Dean do it at the same time?* They hadn't been sitting with us, but there they were, seeking Jesus with their Dad!

Ellie was the only one missing from making the family's dedication to the Lord complete. After observing our commitments for a few weeks, she asked Jesus into her heart, too. All of the Cooper clan was sold out to Jesus!

When Mark was about to graduate from high school, I was talking to the Lord in prayer. I'd been in the construction business with a partner for several years. As I prayed about my sons' futures, I felt as though the Lord was speaking to my heart that I was also going to graduate in two years.

After more prayer and consulting with my pastor and Ellie, my partner approached ME about buying HIM out. We agreed on a price. To my total amazement he came to me with a counter offer after I'd checked the status of our pocketbooks and decided we could swing the deal. His proposal? He wanted to buy ME out for the same sum we'd agreed upon.

Ellie, my Pastor, and I became the three who went to Jesus to seek His advice. "Sell!" We all agreed. Unbelievable! At age 42 I could retire and go into full-time Christian work!

We sought the BIG BOSS'S advice as we traveled through the country to various ministries, wondering where the Lord would have us serve. Nothing seemed to be right until we went to visit my Aunt Ann McClure in New Wilmington, PA. She asked, "Joe, have you seen the new *Bair Foundation* building?"

No, I hadn't, so Ellie and I went to visit Bill Bair who welcomed with the greeting, "Praise the Lord!" as only he can do.

As he began to share his vision for *Family Life America,* something began stirring within both Ellie and my hearts. He laughed as he said, "I told my board we needed a director to work with the families of our foster kids. They told me that there was nothing in the budget for a director of such a job. It would have to be someone who could work without pay."

"We can do that," my answer came. "We can work without any pay," I added.

After booming another— "Praise the Lord!" — we began planning our ministry back in the little town where I'd been baptized as an infant.

At a *Bair Foundation* meeting we were brought up front and the Holy Spirit fell. No questions remained in anyone's mind. We'd experienced the red light to "get ready" for some time, we now had the green light to go full-time for Jesus.

Bill did the obvious thing. He took up a collection for our ministry. $25,000! To us that was the Lord verifying His will for us to work there.

Two years from the exact date that I felt the Lord had told me I was to "graduate too" Ellie and I took over our new office at the *Bair Foundation.*

Family Life America also involved all the Coopers. Ellie and I had the opportunity to watch hundreds of couples renew their commitments to each other and the Lord as we shared with them at *Marriage Encounters*. Teens responded to the love given them at the *Teen Encounters*. We had other meetings with singles and engaged couples. Our ministry was "everyday love and the miracle of oneness to the marriage and family." Our own family relationships blossomed during the twelve years that we served there.

After that, we felt the need to resign to take care of Ellie's aging parents at that time. I agreed with her that we both should respond to their needs according to the scripture in I Timothy 5:8 *"If anyone does not provide for his relatives, and especially for his immediate family, he has denied the faith and is worse than an unbeliever."*

We did that for some time, then I decided that I had a tugging from the Lord to participate in the ministry of friends in India. Arriving in southern India in 1991, I stayed and ministered for six weeks that year.

Dr. Luke, an Indian pastor/evangelist who is also a medical doctor, became one of my brothers-in-Christ in India. After that Dr. Luke wrote me a letter saying, "Your visit to Andhra Pradesh was so blessed to our ministry. Lord has done many wonders and healings by your prayers at the interior village where you have given baptisms. One man by the name of Rajababu had been suffering from T.B. of the spine. He could not stand straight and walk for many years, but after the prayers he is able to stand up and able to walk!

"Another miracle was done at the same place on the same day. One young lady 23 years old whose name is Ganta Devupamma has lost her sight completely six years ago. She could not do her work and was not able to walk due to blindness. But after the prayer, the Lord touched her and healed her.

"Mass healing has taken place and many people have been delivered from devils, healed from headaches, backaches, and ear pains when you prayed on the first day of our convention in the night portion. Glory to God! I have the record with me."

The green light was on again; Ellie remained at home, knowing India has shown itself to be such a fertile field for me. Back in the states I have raised funds to build small churches. Over there a thousand dollars can buy the material for a small church. The natives gladly donate the labor so that they can have a place to go to worship Jesus.

I have continued to return to India each year, having spent nine weeks out of the last fifty-two there. I have witnessed the Holy Spirit perform too many miracles to count in the 24 churches. That is the present count, but the generosity of American Christians is making more churches possible all the time.

It is awesome to see God at work, but my joy came from leading the lost idol worshipers (Hindus) to Jesus. The Lord did not leave my Ellie out. Even though she stayed in the U.S., the Lord stirred 300 Hindus to repent and receive Jesus on Ellie's birthday, as a present to her. Oh, the joy!

There's so much work to do both in American and across the world! Jesus said, *"Behold these words are trustworthy and true. I am coming soon."*

In the meantime, I have found there is no greater thrill than serving the Lord. I only know that each of us needs to heed the lights as I had to do in parachuting. When God's green light comes, we need to jump in with everything we have and give our all to Jesus! His mandate is to GO—"Go ye into all the world and preach the Gospel." Try it-there's no greater reward!

* * * * *

Joe Cooper can be reached at:
Back Yard Ministries
RD #3 Box 139
Kingswood Drive
New Castle, PA 16105

The Lighthouse
The Joy of Restoration

The Pastor George and Nadine Van Riper Story

One of my Sunday School teachers approached me. "I caught Nevin selling drugs today to the other Sunday School students."

The sting of shock penetrated to my bones, then disbelief and bewilderment rocked my spirit. Surely not Nevin! Not my oldest son!

The familiar words of Proverbs 22:6 jutted into my recall. *"Bring up a child in the way he should go and when he is old, he will not depart from it."* This Scripture had meant a lot to me and would again offer comfort; however, at the moment it didn't relieve the devastation that instantly began to erode the foundation of my faith. God's promises are true, but in the reality of life, they sometimes seem a million miles away. This was one of those times.

Nadine and I have been married for 43 years and have three sons. I was saved at fourteen in Pennsylvania. Nadine was saved at twelve. It was the same year, the same month; but she was in West Virginia. I was called to the ministry not long after being saved. I started preaching at sixteen, and I've been in full-time ministry ever since. When one is serving the Lord with all one's heart, what could go wrong?

I found out! We were not aware of any problems with our three boys. While raising them, we trained them in the ways of Jesus. We took them to church from the time they were a few days old. Everything seemed to be going great, then suddenly our family went sour.

We had a ministry in Washington, Pennsylvania, called Soul's Harbor Lighthouse. We were running about 350 in attendance, had a radio-TV ministry spread across the country, and owned our own print shop. I am only saying this to amplify what God did and what can happen in your life. We had property on Interstate 70 — a beautiful 15-acre site with a nice lake in front. We were going to build on it. We had a farm for a rehab program and a Bible school with students from seven different states across the country. We had a great program going.

Family problems seemed nonexistent. That was when one of my Sunday School teachers approached me and said, "Pastor, I have to talk with you."

"What do you want?"

"Well, Brother, I caught Nevin selling drugs today to the Sunday School students."

This news rocked my core. I thought, *Oh my, my son is only fifteen years old!*

I didn't know anything about drugs. I was never a drug addict. I never drank or smoked. Oh, I stole a couple of cigarettes from my grandad and climbed a tree. When I inhaled, I got sick and nearly toppled from the limb. I thought I was going to die! That was enough. I never touched another cigarette. That doesn't mean I was a goody-two-shoes. It means I didn't know anything about drugs or how to handle addiction. Since we didn't have any knowledge of what to do, we went on as normal. We disciplined Nevin and tried to talk to him. But to no avail.

Eventually, he became a drug addict and an alcoholic on the streets of Washington, Pennsylvania.

And here I am a pastor! I thought, *Lord, what's wrong here?*

In 1982 things came to a head, and I resigned as pastor of the Lighthouse Church. When things are going well with a pastor, people are for him; however, when suddenly something goes bananas with a pastor, people jump on him. You have a lot of friends when everything is cool and great and you can say, "Glory to God. I've got victory. I'm successful and prosperous." But when things begin to go haywire, everyone begins to criticize. I had a stack of letters where people told me, "You aren't fit to be in the ministry." I had board members that felt I should resign. They said, "You can't lead a church if you can't lead your family."

There are a lot of parents who have experienced the same thing. People told me, "Well, if you had trained your children right and had lived a good example, they wouldn't have gone astray."

That's not true! We did everything we could, and our boys turned their backs on their teaching and went the way of the world. Two of them in particular. Our youngest son did no offense. He backslid a little but didn't stray in major ways.

Several times, one of our sons nearly got killed. It was because of the company he was keeping. One man chased him with a butcher knife. Had he caught him, his heart would have been lying on the ground. God's hand was on our son and he spared his life.

In 1977 and 1978 I began to have real trauma and emotional problems. When I preached and didn't see my boys coming to God, I blamed God. I said, "God, if you are fair and you're for real, why aren't my boys right with you?"

In 1982 I was at my lowest ebb. I fell apart. I lost my faith in God.

Some said, "You can't believe that. You can't leave the church."

I know what happened to me. I know that deep down in my heart, I really didn't believe God was real. All my life I'd been preaching and saw thousands come to Christ. There I was. The thing that I preached, I didn't believe was real.

That was a difficult thing to handle.

At the time the ministry was running 350 in attendance. All my TV programs got cut off; all radio programs were canceled; we sold the different properties to pay the debts that had arisen; the ministry went into desolution. There was no more.

I thought, *This is the end of things.*

When we left Washington, we thought we would never return. Marriage problems developed, but not on my wife's part. Nadine loved me. For two years our marriage was shaky because of me. I lashed out from the guilt in my heart and my separation from God. I didn't have an anchor. I blamed my wife. I never beat her; I never laid hands on her, but my words hurt her. She went to bed many a night crying. Let me say to wives who have a husband who is messed up, "Keep your faith in God. Hold on to Him."

In the midst of some of my trauma, foolishness, waywardness and anger, Nadine wrote me love letters. I still have some of them. In her letters, she told me how much she loved me. This meant a lot to me.

After I got my life straightened out again, I asked her why she had done that. She explained that she felt it was important to support me by showing me how much she cared.

She held on to God when I had let go.

A lot of pastors are hurting. They are busy, busy, busy.

I didn't notice any signs or symptoms when my boys began doing drugs. Drug abuse was just beginning to get popular. Since it wasn't a prevalent problem, very few parents knew what signs to look for. We didn't know anything about it, so we didn't know what to look for—especially when we didn't realize anything was wrong.

During the time Nevin was experimenting with drugs, we didn't have any problems that would have led to his wanting to. When I discovered his habit, I wondered where he got the money to buy the drugs, but I never asked him. If a person doesn't volunteer information during a testimony, I don't pry. Where and how did Nevin get his drugs? I don't know.

One day we were remodeling the house that we are now living in, and we got a phone call from Nevin. He said, "Dad, I think you'd better come home."

Craig and Melanie, our middle son and his wife, were living in Georgia. We had no idea what they were doing. I didn't know why Nevin wanted us home, but by his voice, I knew something was wrong. We went right home.

Nevin said, "You'd better sit down, Dad."

I did.

He said, "I just got a phone call. Craig and Melanie have been arrested by the Feds for selling drugs in Tennessee."

I gasped. As the story unfolded, my horror grew. This wasn't just state stuff. I said, "Oh, dear Jesus."

The next day we jumped into the car and went down to see Craig. I will never be able to put into words my feeling of despair, hurt, sorrow, and anger when we had to talk to our son through a plate glass window. We couldn't touch him. We couldn't do anything! When we left, we put our hands on the window. He put his hands on the other side. I thought, *God, this is our six-foot-one son, but he is one of the baby boys we cradled in our arms. We took him to Sunday School and church. We had family devotions with him. We prayed everyday for him when he went out the door. God, what went wrong?*

I went on a deep depression trip. I went through the valley of accusation. Why didn't I spend more time with my boys? Why didn't I see these signs? Why didn't I do this? Why didn't I do that? But how did I know to do it?

We went to Craig's hearings, and visited him in prison. He was taken from place to place because they thought a contract was out on his life. We didn't even know where he was a few times. We went down for the hearing when he and Melanie were to be sentenced. We went into the court room in Chattanooga, Tennessee, and waited for our son to be brought down the hall.

We share this testimony many times; but each time we tell it, we live it all over again. We saw our son coming. I started to walk toward him. Nadine went out ahead of me, almost running, intending to put her arms around him.

A Federal marshal stepped in front of her. "Step aside, ma'am. You can't touch him."

Craig was shackled and chained. He moved along with his head down. How could we help—after we had done all we could do?

We sat in the court room that day and heard the gavel crack. We listened to the words, "I sentence you, Melanie Van Riper, to 60 months in a federal prison."

Then my son was sentenced. We heard, "Craig Van Riper, I sentence you to 96 months in a federal penitentiary to be designated at a later date."

I thought, *My God. Eight years of my boy's life is going to be snuffed out.*

Melanie was going to fly there; but we didn't want her to go alone, so we took her. She was committed up in Connecticut. My daughter-in-law and I didn't get along; but when I saw her walk through that gate, I wanted to cry.

As pastors, we all have burdens to carry. The more we serve the Lord, the more the devil is after us. But, thank God, Jesus is always there. When we begin to cave in, that's when we really have to depend on the Lord.

God can restore a pastor. When our two oldest sons drifted away from God and got into deep trouble, we were on the evangelistic field. I agreed to go to a Wednesday night service because it meant so much to my wife.

I said, "This thing isn't for me. God isn't around."

It is important to be in church, whether we're ministering or someone else is ministering to us. On Sunday night we stopped in Richwood, Kentucky, for the service. We didn't know anyone there and had never heard of the pastor, although he was well known. We enjoyed the service very much. At the end the pastor was at the back door shaking hands. He greeted us as we left and said, "Wait a minute. I want to talk to you."

He wanted to know who we were and what we were doing. He said he wanted to pray for us. During the prayer time, he said, "The Lord is showing me that when your sons return, it will be a new beginning for you." He described a few other things including the church that we would be pastoring. Because of all the things that had happened, we didn't know if we even wanted to pastor again.

I said, "That prophecy had to be from the Lord because we hadn't said anything about having sons. We hadn't mentioned our family, so he couldn't have known we had children."

We eventually went back to Washington and started brand new with another church. The very first Sunday Craig and Melanie were there. It was like a new beginning. God blessed us in a beautiful way. It was the first Sunday that Craig was out of prison.

We had lost a 46-acre farm, but in 1987 God restored my ministry in Washington, PA, and in 1996 He gave us a 104-acre farm to run a children's home, a retreat, and a retirement place. We had never had a church building. We had always rented facilities, but in 1997 God made it possible for us to purchase a church just off Interstate 70. You can see it in Washington as you travel the interstate. It's a beautiful piece of property. It's a miracle!

We are now on radio for three hours on Saturday and fifteen minutes every day, Monday through Friday. One of these days we'll be branching out farther. We're on WPIT at 7:30 on the AM dial. On Saturday we're on from nine until twelve noon. We've been on a good while now, and our program is growing. We use all Southern Gospel music. Of course, we use prayer. It is a live show, and we have call-in people who ask for prayer. God has blessed it and used it.

My eldest son, a former drug addict and alcoholic, is now an associate pastor. He is leading other young people to Christ and sharing the love of God. It's beautiful!

We never dreamed that we would come back to Washington to minister, but God has blessed abundantly.

Revival started. The pastor's prophecy in Richwood, Kentucky, ten years earlier, all came true.

We taught our children right from wrong and they knew. They got into trouble and strayed from God; but when they wanted to come back to the Lord, they had the wherewithal to do it. They were aware that I John 1:9 said, *"If we confess our sin, he is faithful and just to forgive our sin and to cleanse us from all unrighteousness."*

There is a victory! Both Craig and Melanie got right with God. When they came out of prison, they began to serve God. They are now working with us in the ministry. The Lord has done a miracle!

There are mothers and fathers and pastors who think there is no hope. But from imprisonment, drug addiction, or whatever, God can bring the family back together. He did it in our family. All our boys are restored and serving the Lord. I pray that the Holy Spirit will move upon the hearts of mothers, dads, pastors and Christian workers. Maybe they are walking through a dark valley. I pray that God will raise them up, increase their faith in the fulfillment of God's promises, and fill them with the truth in His word. I truly believe that if we train children in the way they should go, when they are old, they will not depart from it. Praise the name of the Lord!

* * * * *

The Van Ripers are available to share their story of despair and victory to those who are discouraged or depressed, and need lifted up. We will come on a free-will offering basis and can be contacted by writing to: Pastor George Van Riper, P.O. Box 122, Washington, PA 15301.

Modern-Day Noah

Ray Walters

"No you can't!" Dad told me when I asked to go to my friend Jim's house for the day.

I didn't argue. I simply said, as I turned back to the phone, "I can't come. My father won't let me go."

Anger seared from Dad's eyes as I hung up the receiver. He started after me with a chair raised in the air, but I grabbed hold of it and said in a quiet and very firm voice, "You are NOT going to hit me for telling the truth. How many times have you taught all of us not to lie?" We had locked horns too often, and I couldn't see any reason for his explosion that day. All I could assume was that Dad didn't want Jim's father, a fellow deacon in the church, to know that HE was the reason I couldn't visit his son.

So many times all ten of his children suffered from his overbearing, authoritative anger. I came into the midwestern farm of the Walters family on April 10, 1914. Finances sometimes were tight and problems were many, but Mom never reacted to them like my father did. She always had goodies for us every day when we arrived home from school. She never complained about her own mountain of work. To her four sons and four daughters, she was our own special guardian angel — especially to me. Our unconditional, loving relationship created a wonderful bond with my mother.

I am proud of the fact that I never ever said a cross word to her in the 19 years while living at home. Whenever Dad let his temper go too far, she'd simply drawl, "G e o r g e," in her soft, but firm tone of voice.

For some reason, my father stopped his rages and listened to her. Later I realized there was real love and affection between them. However, this didn't stop Dad from working us too hard - up at 4 a.m. to work in the field, and then we had to milk 15 cows and deliver the milk to the creamery on the way to school. Since I was the oldest of his offspring going to school, I was the driver and I had a late pass from my first class every single day.

After school we had to work in the fields, and then hurry home to milk the cows again. Yes, we were all bone-tired and ready for bed. Our home had five bedrooms. Because I read books until the late hours, the other children refused to sleep in my room. I had to read by an oil lamp since there was no electricity. The 65 books I read every high school semester encouraged me to want to go to college — and to get away from the farm. My father expected all his boys to remain with him, but he knew I didn't intend to stay because I had dreams of college and becoming my own person. All this created a resentment in my father towards me, and I always felt I received more punishment even though I had not committed the infractions he accused me of doing.

While doing such heavy work at the age of 19, I developed a double rupture. It had to be operated on just one month before I had determined to go to college no matter what. I asked my brother to come to the hospital to tell him my plans. I said, "George, I am NOT going home from the hospital! I need to be in Fort Collins to register next week. Will you tell Mother and Dad what I need and what I am determined to go through? I talked my brother into asking Dad for a blank check just to cover my tuition.

After arriving at school, I had not anticipated my financial plight caused by not being able to work for two or three weeks until my incision healed. I'd refused to ask for more on the check which left me with ten dollars for over two weeks. I existed on milk and crackers for more than 14 days. I'd joined a fraternity but was too proud to ask them for help. After school, before I went back to my basement room, I pretended I was eating the goodies in the bakery window next door. I wouldn't recommend this to someone else unless they wanted to go to school as badly as I did.

However, I had the shear joy of knowing I had reached my goal to go to college, which was one of the most satisfying times of my life.

As soon as I was able, I applied for and got not one, but two jobs in a single day - an answer to my prayers. In 1933, a post-depression year, getting any work at all was a great achievement.

One day I went home to visit with a seven dollar pipe in my mouth. "Ray," my mother said, "I'll give you five dollars for that pipe if you'll quit smoking."

Seeing her concern and loving her as I did, I answered, "Mom, here's the pipe. Keep the five dollars. I'll never smoke again." I never did.

Because I wanted so desperately to make something of myself, I studied hard. All through my first year I seemed unfulfilled, and wanting more than four years at Fort Collins, Colorado. After much agonizing, I became determined to go to my uncle's house in Modesto, California. This all seems like someone who did not know what he wanted; but now that I am 84 years old, I know God had a special reason for that move, and kept His watch over my entire life.

Go to my uncle's house? What will I wear? How will I go? Finances made it impossible for me to do anything but hitchhike. My clothes consisted of a beautiful riding pant with flared-out sides, a brand new shining pair of riding boots, and a fancy shirt.

I started from Fort Collins walking toward the Rocky Mountains when a man stopped to ask, "Where are you going?" He picked me up. After we reached his turn-off, he said, "Ray, after talking to you, I feel like giving you some advice. Please give me the clothes you are wearing, and I'll mail them to you later."

He asked me, "Wouldn't you like to come and live with me on my ranch? You will have a good life." I appreciated the offer, but Ray Walters had a mind of his own and a goal. Again I walked. The climb became very steep. I was looking out of a restaurant window, and spotted a man at the gas pump. Hurriedly, I approached him for a ride across Rabbit Ear Pass. "Are you a good driver?" he asked. I regretted every minute of that terrible ride across the mountains. He was very drunk, so I had to pull him off the dashboard many times.

In a small town across the mountains, I spotted a railroad station. With all the courage I could muster, I approached a boxcar where some rough-looking men were boarding. When they spotted me, they yelled, "You'd better come on if you want to ride this train." It had already begun to move. I threw my bag in the door. Someone had to pull me up. I quickly receded to the farthest corner away from the other characters. I never told my mother about this trip; she would have really been worried. In fact, I was very uneasy. I pretended I was asleep, with one eye on the others. Bumpy, bumpy! Oh, I never dreamed I could get myself into such a horrible situation. I never gave up.

The most embarrassing time of my life came next when the police herded us into a holding complex, and stripped our clothes to be fumigated. We were kept there until morning. Please, never again.

I then began to walk toward California. As I walked around the Great Salt Lake, it was very hot. Exhausted, I collapsed in a heap on the ground beside the road until I realized a man was standing over me, "Are you all right?"

After asking my destination, he said, "Get in." It was so hot, many women wrapped their feet in cloth to keep from burning their soles. This kind man said he could take all of them. He'd slow down, then look back until he saw the ladies had been picked up. This was another good Samaritan man God put in my path to watch over me on my trip. So kind, he refused to turn toward his home in Sacramento but turned and drove me all the way to Modesto, California to my uncle's door.

I believed as a boy that because I went to church and graduated from catechism class, I was saved and would go to heaven. My life was never without God being involved in my plans, which was due to my precious mother. However, as I grew older, I realized I was missing something more precious, *"The peace that passeth all understanding."* Two friends in San Diego, California, kept asking me many questions. For a period of one year I attempted to answer. After I wore my small pocket Bible almost out, I came alive. I was baptized and came up shouting a loud "Hallelujah" four times. After the clapping and voices subsided, I shouted, "Praise the Lord!"

I embarked on a journey the rest of my life - one filled with challenges, hurts, joys, and sorrows, but then I knew, that I knew, that I was saved. It is wonderful to know that I am in God's will! I'm happier than I've ever been in my life because God has shown me the difference between happiness and joy. Also I have learned how really BIG God is!

Mama died. To my surprise my father was greatly affected by her death. It made me see him through different eyes. Once when I'd confronted him about my beatings, saying, "You never loved me, ever hugged me, or told me you loved me," tears welled up in his eyes. "I only did it to make you learn and teach you about life. I did it because I loved you," he said.

I thought, *that's a strange form of love*, but somehow I think he did love us. After Mom's death, he mellowed. It amazed me that he missed her so much. So did I. But life goes on. I married and adopted a beautiful daughter, who is my pride and joy.

I went many places and had unforgettable experiences, but I couldn't believe it when I wound up in Charlotte, North Carolina, and was offered the opportunity to open "Noah's

Toy Shoppe" on the PTL Club grounds. In later years after the demise of PTL, I was going to play the role of a "Modern-Day Noah."

That store gave me so many blessings. Folks came from all over the country, bubbling with enthusiasm of how the PTL Club had brought them to Jesus.

We made the store look like Noah's Ark, and we had stuffed animals of all kinds, including learning toys with no violence aboard my ship. Far more important were the humans who came in and shared their stories about Jesus' love and His blessings. My greatest joy was to be involved with God's Special Children plus meeting and becoming friends with the most loving and gentle man I had ever met, Uncle Henry Harrison.

I often thought of how my mother and father would have been thrilled to see me in the center of such Christian activity — especially Mama.

Even though I was having a glorious time sharing Jesus aboard the Ark, I began to hear rumors that the PTL had lost its bearings and was set on a course destined for destruction.

The news of their scandal of corruption and deception hit the media on a Monday morning, and I felt as though my own ship would lose its moorings there on the PTL grounds. During months of agony and working with the stores and bankruptcy, it became apparent PTL's demise would come shortly.

Margia and I were hurt, the employees were hurt, and many Christians throughout America were sorely hurt. Everyone felt PTL had been a great tribute to Jesus. "Somehow, Lord," I prayed, "people need to know that, despite the problems, PTL brought hope and joy to many people."

At age 82 it no longer mattered what had taken place back on the farm when I was a child, but the thing that meant most to me was showing the world what GOOD had come out of the PTL Club.

I sent out requests for people to write me about how

they had been blessed in spite of the failures. Romans 8:28 became my mainstay. *"All things work together for good to all those who love the Lord and are called according to His purpose."* Many had loved the Lord and been called through Heritage, USA.

Somehow God let me know not to write what others have written, but to tell God's side (the Good Side). I believed the scandal had given Jesus and the Christians a black eye; and through the hand of Jesus, I wanted to help heal the damage. Folks found salvation and healing and fellowship at PTL or through the television show, work shops, seminars, the Upper Room, and the daily teachings to thousands of people, began opening up their hearts and sharing what the Lord had accomplished via the ministry.

As Noah did, I reached out with my olive branch. I sought peace and reconciliation for everyone - the staff and the givers. It worked. Not only did others find reconciliation by sharing their joys and blessings, but as a Modern-Day Noah, I'd found peace and hope, by the help of God, by putting many of their stories into a book called *"Diamonds in the Rough - Hidden Treasures of PTL."* Margia and I found healing balm, as the book has become a book of healing to those who were criticized for giving or coming.

The book *"Diamonds in the Rough - Hidden Treasures of the PTL"* is for you. May it be a hand of healing that reaches from one heart to another, bringing forgiveness, reconciliation, and peace.

At age 84 I am excited beyond measure, and I owe it all to God whom I serve with a glad heart.

The following are excerpts from letters received about *Diamonds in the Rough* which have thrilled my soul.

One came from San Antonio, TX. It said: "I have read the first three chapters of your book and been reduced to many tears already! It is truly a gift that will touch many lives. I'm looking forward to reading all of it. What a blessing you have been in many lives and with this book you are reaching so many others."

And the crowning glory came from beloved "Aunt" Susan Harrison, Uncle Henry's widow. She wrote:

"Hidden Treasures are now revealed and have enriched lives everywhere. You and *Diamonds in the Rough* together will remain a treasure to many for years to come."

The book has truly made me a "Modern-Day Noah!"

* * * * *

Diamonds in the Rough may be ordered by calling 803-548-7718 or writing 107 Cedar Hollow, Fort Mill, SC 29715.

The Provider

Ravenel Scott

My brother and I, dressed in our Sunday best, stood with our father watching the huge black Buick come down the dusty road to our house. Little did we know on that autumn day in 1932 at the ages of 9 and 10, that our lives would change forever.

Few memories remain for me of those early years on our sharecropper's tobacco and cotton farm in Hemingway, SC, but one stands out in my mind as though it were painted in oil on canvas to last forever. One day my mother was cooking when she suddenly put her hand to her head and cried, "Oh! My head aches!" She had experienced a stroke at the young age of thirty-nine. I was the one who sat for hours beside her bed, running errands at her request so often that my brothers called me "Mama's pet."

One day my father was in the bedroom shaving when Mother asked for a mirror. She raised her head from the pillow, straightened her hair, smiled, then gently laid back down. She was gone. I have always felt she was concerned about appearing before Jesus and wanted to look her best.

Our father called his six children together and told us, "Some of you will have to live with other people, but they will take care of you and love you." He explained that he simply could not take care of such a big flock since Mama was gone and the Great Depression was upon us.

(Later in life my father gave me a special gift that Mama

had asked him to save for me. It was a Smith & Wesson, pearl handled, 35MM hand gun that had been given to her by her father. This cherished gift occupies a peaceful place in the night stand by my bed.)

With broken and fearful hearts, my brother and I entered into that ominous black sedan and began the long journey to Connie Maxwell Orphanage, (Now Children's Home), near Greenwood, SC. Our first automobile ride was a far cry from our journeys to town with my father. He'd hitch up a huge mule to a wagon, then call, "Let's go!" and we'd all pile on. Our return trips always came after dark with some of us and our father dozing at the reins, but that mule would always find his way home!

Before we arrived at Connie Maxwell, we were told some of its history. A seven-year-old girl named Connie died of scarlet fever in 1883. Her parents, the Maxwells, were so broken-hearted that they decided to build the orphanage in her honor on a 480 acre tract of land. Later on, the Southern Baptists assumed the responsibility for supporting this great work, which they still continue to do.

When my brother J.D. and I stepped out of that big Buick, we faced the largest building we'd ever seen; and then we became members of the largest family we'd ever known. The building, known as Number 5, had about 20 rooms on three levels and housed 20 boys, one cottage mother, one young girl to help her, plus a school teacher who lived on the second floor.

Thoughts of Connie Maxwell today bring to me an overwhelming sense of gratitude - gratitude to the Lord for His concern and provision for my care; to the cottage mother, Miss Knight, who, by some miracle, managed to keep peace among 20 boys and take care of their daily needs; to my mentor and substitute father, Jack Sheridon, who took us under his wing. He taught me the fundamentals of the printing trade and helped me grow in the discipline of becoming a man at the same time.

By far my greatest blessing was that, in another building similar to where I was staying, a young girl was growing into womanhood. Her name was Jennie Loftis, and she later became my wife and lifelong companion.

My most vivid remembrance during those Great Depression years were on the occasions, especially Thanksgiving time, when railroad cars would roll in filled with all kinds of produce — gifts from farmers, churches, and individuals, given from caring hearts to the children.

How exciting it was to swarm into the box cars to transport the provisions to the storage houses, one of which was the basement of the printing department building. Later we discovered an unlocked window which gave us a secret food supply for campfire excursions into the deep woods behind the dairy farm. We'd often raid the hen house for eggs and the storage room for canned pork brains or salmon, build a fire, and enjoy scrambled brains or salmon and eggs. Later in life I discovered the high cholesterol content of brains and eggs; however, that combination stayed my favorite breakfast or campfire dish.

Our source dried up suddenly when Mr. Sheridan, a good detective as well as a printer, lifted my foot while I was operating a press and matched my shoe to the footprints formed below the basement window. I don't remember the penalty for stealing supplies, but there was no such thing as an allowance, there were no TV's to be deprived of, and a child couldn't be sent to his room alone because it had to be shared with 20 others. The usual punishment was more chores. If our "Crime" merited it, we'd be sent to Dr. Jamison, the Superintendent. Few of us ever had to report to him.

The mystery remains as to how they were able to keep so many in line. Only once was I confronted with Miss Knight and her hickory switch. For some infraction, I was summoned to her room. While holding one hand, she applied the stinging switch to my bare legs as I pranced around and around trying to get away. Today's parents wouldn't use a switch for fear of being arrested for child abuse, but one switching brought a change in my behavior. Perhaps if "sparing the rod and spoiling the child" were in vogue today, we wouldn't see school children shooting friends and parents.

Dr. Jamison also served as pastor of our church. A Godly man, he personified the father authority figure. Very kind and caring, he elicited awe and respect. These factors have to be the secret to his success for so many years, beginning at Connie Maxwell in 1900 at the age of 36 and continuing until 1946. A tall, graying man with a goatee, he was always formally dressed.

Every Sunday we were all required to dress up in our Sunday best and go to Sunday School. Under Dr. Jamison's preaching, I was introduced to Jesus at the age of twelve when I accepted Him in my heart by faith. I still cherish the Bible the superintendent presented to me personally upon my graduation in 1940. The verse he signed inside was from II Timothy 2:1: *"Thou, therefore, my son, be strong in the grace that is in Christ Jesus."* I will always be grateful to God for bringing me under the influence and care of A.T. Jamison and Connie Maxwell Children's Home.

In 1940 a dark war cloud rolled across Europe and Asia and eventually crossed the Atlantic and Pacific to dump its rain upon the United States. It happened just at the time I received my diploma from Greenwood High School and received a "Godspeed farewell" from Connie Maxwell. Suddenly I was launched into the larger world of college, career opportunities, family responsibilities, and World War II. Sam Smith, the superintendent's assistant, was instrumental in securing a part-time job for me with Keys Printing Company and helped me register at Furman University, both located in Greenville, SC.

The first year was extremely stressful and busy. My days were consumed with classes, study, work and sleep, leaving little time for recreation. At Keys Printing I became a linotype operator because of my training at Connie Maxwell's print shop.

At that time war drums began to beat with greater urgency, and men were either being drafted or enlisting in the armed services. We were told that we could remain in college if we enlisted in the reserves. Most of us signed on the dotted line and remained in our classes until that infamous day when Japan bombed Pearl Harbor. Instantly we were at war, and the call came for all of us to report for testing and assignment NOW!!

We were given the opportunity to apply for officer training and be tested for classification. I chose to be tested for Air Corp Cadet training. If I could pass the test and complete the training, I would earn the rank of a 2nd Lieutenant, a boost in pay from $35 to $110 a month.

A prime reason for my decision was that my sweetheart, Jennie, had graduated from Connie Maxwell and had moved to Greenville as a telephone operator for Southern Bell. This gave us more time to see each other and get serious about marriage.

Cadet training offered many challenges for me to stretch my body and mind to their limits. The most stress came at the end of my twelfth week of an eighteen-week advanced training at Selma Field, Louisiana, on Saturday, April 8, 1944. The outcome of a four-hour exam that morning would disqualify me for cadet training or assure me of my 2nd Lt. commission.

Adding to that pressure was the excitement permeating in my heart. Jennie was to arrive by bus from Greenville at noon. Our plan was to be married that afternoon, and I so wanted to present my anticipated commission to her as a gift. How I prayed for God's blessings. He must have had His hand in all of that, for I scored 95 on the test and Jennie arrived right on time.

That great moment when it all came together set the course for the rest of my life. With Jennie by my side, the Lieutenant bars on my shoulders, and God's hand leading me, I was ready to fight the war, continue my printing career, and rear a family.

After we were married, I was transferred to Pueblo, Colorado, where apartments were scarce. In desperation, I approached a widow at the USO club. She said she had a room in her house that we might have, but she must ask one question, "Do you have any bed bugs in your luggage?" Regardless of her perception of Southerners, she became a gracious hostess and we became like family.

After Pueblo I was sent to Panama City, Florida, for gunnery training and then assigned to the Air Force base in Lincoln, Nebraska, where four officers and six enlisted men formed a B24 bomber crew that would spend the rest of the war together as a combat team. Our mission? "Destroy the enemy and stay alive."

In September of 1944 I was one of 40,000 airmen leaving Norfolk, Virginia, on Liberty ships to join the 15th Air Force in Italy. After 28 hazardous days of taking evasive action to avoid the prying eyes of German U-boats, we arrived in Naples. During that trip it was reassuring and exciting to see a great number of Navy destroyers and cruisers moving in and out of the 100-ship convoy performing their protective mission.

Upon our arrival in Naples, we were given a 24-hour leave before boarding the train for the week-long trip over the mountains to Bari. Here we were to become the 64th bomber group with missions into Czechoslovakia, Hungary, Austria, and Germany.

My combat experience lasted 6 months and included 35 missions, the number necessary to be transferred back to the States for R & R. We completed our last mission one day before V-day in Europe in 1945.

Many close encounters with death and tragic losses of entire crews took place as planes were destroyed in the air by German fighters or anti-aircraft fire. One of the first tragedies for me was news that my best friend and best man who had been assigned to a B17 in England was shot down and killed on his first raid.

The first time our squadron of 32 planes lined up for takeoff on an early winter morning, tragedy struck. The lead plane, fully loaded with four 500 pound bombs, ten men, and 2,700 gallons of high octane gasoline, was gaining speed for lift off when it suddenly turned its nose and exploded. In about ten minutes the only remains of the plane, bombs, and men was a large black mark on the runway. That brought to all of us, in stark reality, that we were really at war. Was the tragedy caused by mechanical or human failure? In my assessment there was no difference. My mission was serious, and that experience gave me the determination to do my work to the ultimate of my ability, but it also strengthened my need for my God.

Gathered in the briefing room that early morning in January of 1945, we received our target information before the sun was up. Heaviness loomed in the air because of the rumors that a very special and dangerous mission was planned for that day.

We learned our target would be ball bearing factories in Augsburg, Germany. Knowing ball bearings to be essential to the German war machine, we hoped to destroy or cripple the plants.

The plan was for the squadron to peal off once we arrived at the target area and cross the initial point of the bomb run individually, so that each bombardier would be able to direct the bombs to individual targets, rather than have the usual mass bombing.

That plan also placed each plane on its own, giving the anti-aircraft gunners single targets on which to concentrate. Mountainous Augsburg was located about 10,000 feet high, thus giving the anti-aircraft guns a much closer target than normal.

Our plane, being about tenth in line, gave those enemy gunners plenty of time to adjust their sights and determine the height of the explosions. They were right on target. So were we!

During the bomb run, the bombardier controlled the plane holding it as steady as possible so that the bombsight could direct the bombs to the target. We didn't have smart bombs like those of today! Once our bombs left the plane, they were on their own; and the pilot was free to resume control and take any evasive action needed to prevent more damage by anti-aircraft shells or hostile fighter planes.

During that five-minute bomb run, 88mm shells were exploding all around us. Bursts came close enough to shake the plane and pepper the fuselage with shrapnel. One piece pierced the pilot's windshield, hitting the co-pilot's left arm so badly that only one muscle held it together. One large piece penetrated the instrument panel about a foot away from my back.

More reports came over the intercom about other hits, but ours were the most serious. During those few bomb-riddled minutes I was huddled with one flak suit under me, another around my body, and a helmet pulled down tight upon my head.

I kept praying with an urgency, "Lord, PLEASE protect me and bring me through this ordeal. I promise if you save me, I'll commit myself to a lifetime of service to you." He had my undivided attention!

Yet our problems weren't over. After we left the field of fire, the wounded co-pilot kept pleading, "Help!"

The bombardier, who had done his job well by hitting the target, made his way through the cramped crawl space to the cockpit in order to take care of his secondary job of official crew medic. He was so shaken that he was unable to administer the morphine for the pain or apply the tourniquet to stop the bleeding.

Flak had broken the windows in my compartment and destroyed some electrical cables controlling the cockpit instrument panel, causing the engine to "runaway." The result? A scary loss of power and altitude.

Hearing the desperate pleas of his co-pilot, the pilot ordered me to come and help him. I gave him a shot of morphine and applied a tourniquet. The poor guy was stretched out on the cockpit floor for the four-hour trip back to base.

No other crew member had been injured, but the plane continued to lose altitude.

The pilot ordered, "Dump all ammo, flak suits, guns, and anything not bolted down." This drastic measure was meant to hold altitude since the engines were still not fully under control and were not producing enough power to maintain necessary speed.

Once I was back at my post, the pilot cried, "Give me a position report and direct me to Switzerland," which was the closest possible base unless we landed on enemy territory.

Because of the reduced weight, the engines started to perform well enough to maintain altitude of about 10,000 feet.

Consulting my G Box and Loran directive system as well as some pinpoints on the ground, I was able to determine our location and set a course to Switzerland. The crew and I decided we would love to have a vacation in neutral Switzerland!

Unable to rejoin our formation, we found ourselves alone in the sky over Germany with a crippled plane and a severely injured co-pilot. The danger of being spotted by enemy fighters and ground anti-aircraft added to our perilous situation.

A blizzard began to block our vision and snow sprayed all over the maps I was consulting on my lap board. According to my calculations, we were crossing the Alps. The pilot asked, "What's the tallest mountain in this area?"

Upon reporting, "Some peaks were 11,000 feet high," he responded, "That's just great! We're now below 10,000 feet."

Coming out of the storm, we could see the snow-covered ground. A river below with peculiar twists gave me a positive pinpoint of our location.

The engine began to perform better, causing us to gain in altitude, so the pilot asked for a direction to return us to our base in Italy. Spotting a possible hot spot for anti-aircraft guns on my map, I informed the pilot, "You'd better dog-leg and avoid that area."

Seeing another plane crossing that area, the pilot told me, "Take it easy! I'm going to follow them."

The gunners on the ground let him go by but decided to turn all the guns loose as we flew over, hitting the fuselage, but we escaped more serious damage. That encounter made the pilot give up the idea of following the other plane and decide to take my directions.

For four hours we were able to hold our altitude to about 2,000 feet over the Adriatic Sea. The pilot commanded us, "Keep your life jackets on and be ready to bail out at a moment's notice." With the controls out, we had no idea how much fuel we had left.

We needed to land at a special hospital base so that our co-pilot could receive quick treatment. As we approached the runway, the pilot reported, "I'll maintain 2,000 feet until we reach the runway, then I'll drop quickly just in case we run out of fuel on the approach." His precautions were justified. The engines quit at the end of the runway! We didn't even have enough fuel to turn off!

Later in life, while sharing this experience with a preacher friend and voicing how upset I'd been by the pilot's decision not to make the dog-leg that I felt would have kept us from an additional anti-aircraft attack, he asked me, "How much time would the dog-leg have added to the trip?"

After I told him, "about twenty minutes," he observed, "It must have been God's providential care for if you had done the dog-leg and taken that 20 minutes more, the crew, the plane, and you could have been lost in the Adriatic." God DOES come in unexpected ways and times!

Our combat mission, along with the opportunity to explore ancient Italy and learn its history, opened my eyes to our greater mission. This soldier found himself thousands of miles from home engaged in a great freedom effort. The greater mission was to keep this freedom alive, to enjoy the whole world with all its wonders, to unveil the mysteries of the universe, and to have access to the God of all there is through His Son, Jesus Christ. We are to protect the rights of all people - to participate in the same mission.

On May 7, 1945, the war came to an end in Europe. Even though Japan had not surrendered, I'd flown my last combat mission, attained my new rank of 1st Lt. and received orders to return to the States.

Our crew was to fly our B24 to the U.S. by way of Africa and the Azores, then land in Bangor, Maine. From there I was transferred to Houston, Texas, to await orders to the Japanese theatre.

With a grateful heart, while awaiting that call, we learned that the war was over. President Truman had decided to drop the atomic bomb which ended the Second World War.

Life began to escalate as I began to establish a career and family. I also strived in earnest to fulfill my commitment to the Lord made that day 25 thousand feet over Germany. Abandoning thoughts of college, I returned to Keys to continue my printing career.

Determination and love for the work propelled me into greater responsibility. After eight years of jobs ranging from linotype operator to pressman, I became plant manager with the responsibility of overseeing 75 people.

Printing technology was in a fast-forward, revolutionary change. My life became full of learning experiences. Linotype was being replaced by the computer. The flatbed letterpress was being relegated to the antique heap by the offset press. Laborious hand-operations of the bookkeeper and production control personnel were being taken over by the computer.

While establishing my career and home, I had little time to fulfill my promise to the Lord. Jennie and I joined Pendleton Street Baptist Church, but we were not regular attenders.

On March 5, 1950, life changed dramatically when our daughter, Linda Gayle, arrived. Still wanting to maintain our life style, Jennie and I decided she and our baby would benefit most if Mother and daughter could be together day by day. We never regretted our decision. How grateful we are for the wonderful bond between my daughter and her mother.

Desiring to further our relationship with the Lord and establish our daughter in church led us to membership in Northgate Baptist Church in 1952.

We'd only been there for about a year when they asked me to lead a Sunday School class, and later I was ordained a deacon.

Although I had accepted the Lord at age 12, taken a one-year Bible course at Furman University, joined Northgate and became a deacon, I was NOT prepared for the responsibility of teaching others about Jesus. My inadequacies sent me on a quest to study the Bible which I combined with much prayer.

Events in my life revealed what it means to be "In Christ," and see His will fulfilled. One such event took place in 1962 when I'd become so caught up in my job that I was working 12 to 15 hours a day. A fungus had attacked my lung, one that I had contracted while playing with pigeons behind the print shop at Connie Maxwell. It had remained dormant until my immune system, being overworked, broke down.

The fungus destroyed a lobe of my lung which had to be removed surgically. After that I was transferred to the National Institute of Health in Bethseda, Maryland, for treatment.

There the prescribed grueling and painful treatment lasted four months, but the remaining fungi were destroyed. This good news combined with Jennie's supportive weekly visit, helped me to fully recover. Back at Keys Printing, I resolved to continue my printing career and renewed my determination to fulfill my commitment to the Lord.

It is while doing His work affecting the lives of hurting people that I feel closest to Him. On one occasion while visiting a young abandoned mother of two in Asheville, NC, we noticed many pictures of Jesus on the walls. Her despair and hopelessness appearing on her face as she held one of her children made it obvious that she did not know the real Jesus portrayed by the pictures. It was a joy to see the transformation in her as we explained that Jesus was really the only One who could come into her life and give her hope. In prayer, I believe she accepted Him and let Him come in by faith.

On another occasion, while sitting on a bare floor in an empty house with a young mother and her two children, I experienced that ministering presence of Jesus.

The husband and father had left them to pursue his own desires with no consideration for their welfare. Praying for their reconciliation and God's grace, I was led to find the father and persuade him to return to his family. Seeing them together again gave me renewed awareness of what God can accomplish through the obedience of a committed servant.

Then again there was that advertising executive who broke into tears when he, in desperation and hope, accepted Jesus as his Lord and Savior - exemplifying the universal need for a saving and personal relationship with Jesus.

My own personal relationship with the Lord began to increase when I was contemplating retirement at age 62, after owning Scott Press for two years. Selling it and working for another printing company for 15 years, I received a midnight call from Dr. James Thompson. "Jimmy," beloved founder and operator of Christian TV Station WGGS and Faith Printing Company, he asked, "Would you like to come to work at Faith Printing as a salesman?"

God's hand had to have been at work, for my only previous contact with him had been through some dealings with his printing company. I accepted and began a 10-year adventure dealing with many dedicated and devout men and women of God.

Helping writers and publishers of inspirational literature gave me the opportunity to be a part of the Lord's great evangelistic effort. Stories of God at work in people's lives all over the world through Son-Rise and other publishers have inspired me to greater heights in service to Him.

That work brought Jim and Florence Biros of New Wilmington, PA, into my life. Florence's joy was Son-Rise Publications; Jim's was a dietary supplement - "Green Supreme with Barley Power."

The barley leaf grown on Western Pennsylvania farms, however, has played a major role in my effort to develop and maintain a new healthy lifestyle. That came about when I was preparing to go to the National Religious Broadcasting Convention in Washington, DC, to advertise the capabilities of Faith Printing Company in producing inspirational books.

A trip to my doctor made me think about my trip more seriously when he said, "Your body doesn't have the stamina to go. Your blood pressure is much too high. Your diabetic tendency and blood sugar are both out of control. You need to lose at least fifty pounds." Besides all that, my hiatal hernia was being affected by gastric problems and arthritic pains were restricting my movement. Drastic steps needed to be taken.

Armed with some medication and prayer, I spent the next week at NRB for Faith Printing, but I went into a rigorous lifestyle change involving healthy food and exercise when I returned home. At that time I began supplementing my diet with four barley power tablets a day.

Reading all I could find about diet and health and maintaining a tight rein on my eating and exercise habits, I was able to bring my problems under control. In six months I dropped 50 pounds, brought the blood sugar level down without insulin, eliminated the gastric problems, resolved the arthritic pain, and began lowering my blood pressure.

Along with my doctor's prescription and advice, I attribute much of that success to a right pattern of eating and exercise. I am convinced that without the nutritional benefits of green barley leaves, my transformation into a healthy human being could not have been accomplished. I stress all this because I know how difficult it is to live a happy and fulfilled life when your health is bad.

After my six- month health regimen I was able to experience a life-changing experience on a trip to India. One of my customers, Dr. Richard Belcher, a theologian at Columbia Bible College in Columbia, SC, invited me to accompany him on a mission trip to India to visit M.A. Thomas and support the great work of God there. During 35 years of evangelistic work in India, M.A. Thomas had founded 350 churches, 65 religious-oriented schools, 7 seminaries, 5 orphanages, and 2 hospitals, which were mainly supported by churches in the United States.

During our 13-day visit to participate in a pastoral convention in KOTA, I witnessed firsthand God at work among the people in the leper colonies, in the slums of Bombay, where more than 200 believers worshipped with us in an area church. We were all touched by the transforming work of the Holy Spirit.

Such an experience propelled me into a more intimate relationship with Christ who I've seen is at work in all the world and in the heart of everyone who calls Him "Lord."

The life God gave me seventy-five years ago along with the new one He gave me by the Holy Spirit continues to grow and expand. He continues to open up new avenues of service. For the past 10 years Jennie and I have led a Bible study and worship service at Pendleton Manor, a retirement care center in Greenville. Great joy comes to us as we encourage those who are separated from their families. Until the Lord calls them home, they will not lose fellowship with other believers and Christ.

I have absolutely no regrets about my committment to serve Christ so many years ago. He lifted me out of that tobacco farm; provided my care at Connie Maxwell; gave me my wonderful life-mate, Jennie; saved me from almost certain death during the war; provided a rewarding career; and entrusted me with the ministry of teaching the Gospel of Jesus Christ.

My deeper feeling is one of overwhelming gratitude to God for His universal love and for the promise of a personal relationship with Christ to all who will come to Him. My conviction is that the human spirit will never be satisfied until it finds fellowship on a personal level with God. Many mysteries remain concerning God's plan for us. *"Now we are but a poor reflection' then we shall see face to face. Now I know in part; then I shall know fully, even as I am fully known."* (I Corinthians 13:12).

There have been times when I have doubted my salvation and floundered in my quest for the assurance of being in His will. However, He has seen fit to reveal to me through the Bible, His Spirit, and a lifetime of service, the secrets to a happy and fulfilling life in Him. He is Jehovah Jirah, the Great Provider.

* * * * *

A. Ravenel Scott is retired and lives with his wife in Greenville, SC.

Lorraine Who?

Lorraine Lewis

Music consumed me from the time I was a little girl. By the age of seven, I was appearing on country music shows, singing my heart out. Later I sang with big bands. My dreams focused on my special talent. I was a SINGER!

Even though I married and had two adorable daughters, I never gave up my lifelong dream of being a professional singer. Nothing exhilarated me more than going down to my husband's bar and letting the spotlight shine on me as I sang. When my girls were raised, I planned to go out and step up to microphones across the country and receive the applause I felt my talent deserved.

In 1969 I was confronted with a surprising pregnancy, but thoughts of snuggling with a baby in my arms enticed me. When a nine-pound baby girl arrived, she immediately became the family's darling "Buffy."

Her two older sisters and I doted on her, and we were all devastated when we learned she had physical problems. When she was ten months old, I took her to the Cleveland Clinic for tests and diagnosis.

My thoughts the night before the doctors were to tell us the results were interrupted by the jangle of the telephone.

Mom's welcome voice came through loud and clear, as if she were standing right beside me instead of calling long-distance from Florida to Ohio.

"Lorraine, you need to call on the Lord to help you through this," she said.

I welcomed her concern, but I didn't want to hear the implication that there might be something terribly wrong with my Buffy, so I ended the conversation with these words to my mother, "If they say my baby's going to die, don't even mention God to me again."

After hanging up the phone, I pondered her words. My own father had died when I was quite young. Later Mom married a Baptist preacher, and my sister had become the wife of an Assembly of God minister. They had a lot of faith, but mine was so lacking that if I tried to contact Him, the Lord would have had to say, "Lorraine? -- Lorraine who?"

Before I visited the clinic the next day, I tried to steel myself for what their professionals might say. Even with the mind preparation I'd made, I was not prepared for what they had to say. "Your daughter has a rare form of Muscular Dystrophy called Werdnig-Hoffmans Disease." After that they went on to describe the prognosis.

I began to realize that they were trying to tell me that my darling Buffy was suffering from a terminal disease.

"Are you saying that my baby's going to die?" I asked.

"Not right away. We give her two to four years to live."

My own response startled even me. "With God's help, we will raise her." Such a surprising statement for someone who claimed no faith in the Lord!

Words cannot express the depth of my feelings as I cuddled my infant against me on the way home. When we followed a school bus, my mind and heart tore at my very being. Dear, darling Buffy might never make it to school!

In the months that followed, a drastic change came about in my plans for the future. As I watched the little child we all adored struggle to function, my aspirations for personal fame and fortune diminished so much that I had no desire to go to my husband's nightclub, let alone sing there.

As I hovered over my sleeping child, I'd ask myself, "Wouldn't you rather be a good mother to her while she's still yours than pursue a career in music?" No doubt lingered in my mind. She came first.

My brother-in-law pastor kept assuring me, "I keep praying that Buffy will be healed."

As her mother, I was willing to try anything to have my little girl get better. People from the local Assembly of God invited us to join them. I went and took all three of my girl. The whole church welcomed us with open arms.

When I heard of a man, an American Indian that had a ministry in Michigan, we traveled there just to have Rev. Plane pray for Buffy.

One time the Indian minister was in our area. We invited him to visit and then I gave my heart to Jesus by confessing my sins and asking for forgiveness as this man, Rev. Plane, prayed with and for me. That day changed the course of my life.

The years ahead were not easy. Buffy suffered many physical setbacks and was hospitalized many times. The bond between her and me was one so binding that it was as if her umbilical cord had never been cut at birth.

She struggled to do anything physical; but she accepted the Lord into her own heart at the age of eight. Buffy never ceased smiling or trying to conquer her physical handicaps.

Her father left, but later I met a man named Bill. I met him through Buffy. His own son had drowned at the age of thirteen, and he was struggling to find meaning for his own existence. His sister had met us where she worked and she'd told Bill, "You need to meet this little girl and her family. They have something we don't have."

She didn't know it then, but it didn't take us long to share with Bill and his sister that special ingredient that made it possible for us to cope with all of Buffy's problems - His name is Jesus. Regardless of all the outer circumstances, He was the source of the peace we had inside that made us joyful on the outside. "Behold, I make all things new."

Buffy was hospitalized many times. At the age of fifteen, she was struggling so much in an oxygen tent just to breathe that the doctors came to me and said, "You have to go in there and tell her that you are letting her go. She's hanging on just for you."

My daughter Beth was with me. We walked into the room and saw Buffy lying on her right side in the oxygen tent. As I looked at her laboring for every breath she took, I asked the Lord what right this doctor had to tell me that I had to tell my daughter she was going to die when we all three there in that room knew that our faith would bring her through.

I unzipped the tent and leaned down to her ear. Her eyes were closed. What would I do without this precious angel in my life? I whispered in her ear, "Buffy, the doctors tell me that you are very ill and that you may not make it." Then I could not finish what I had started to say. I changed my words and I said, "Buffy, if you have the strength to fight this one more time, I know the Lord will see you through it." I told her if she was too tired to fight it, that was all right too. I had a brief conversation with her of how we would all be together in Heaven one day anyway. As I finished my little speech, she opened her eyes and said to my daughter, "Would you just tell Mom I'm gonna be fine." We prayed all night, it seemed.

The next morning the doctor came into the room and examined her. He said, "I don't know how, but she's going to make it. He said that she had been literally drowning in her own fluid.

Buffy lived nearly three more years after that. The little girl that they said would not live to go to school graduated in 1986 with a straight "A" average in just 11 years. She was just 5 weeks shy of her 18th birthday when she went home to be with the Lord. The Lord presented me with a new grandson on her birthday.

In those 18 years Buffy had pneumonia 17 times. Each time the Lord brought her through. She had a mission here. She touched a lot of lives. The doctors said that pneumonia would probably take her, but it didn't.

She died in my arms in the privacy of our home. Her lungs just gave out and she very peacefully went to sleep. I had time to explain to her that we would miss her very much, but in heaven it would seem as quick as turning a page and we would be there with her.

Just before she died, she opened her eyes very wide and said, "Wait a Minute. What's wrong? What's wrong?" I believe with all my heart, that at that moment, she saw Jesus.

Buffy

At birth you named me "Buffy"
   When they laid me in your lap.
But I'd have another title;
   I'd be known as handicapped.

You told me everyone is handicapped
   In one way or another.
I soon learned for every special child,
   God gives a special mother.

When I learned that I was handicapped
   And I would never walk,
You pointed out the good things;
   I still could see and talk.

Walking isn't everything,
   That's what you used to say,
And as long as we're together,
   You'd be my strength each day.
Remember?

They said I'd never go to school;
    You said that wasn't true.
In fact I've done a lot of things
    They said I'd never do.

We've shared a lot of secrets,
    Some good ones and some bad,
And no one can ever take away
    The memories that we've had.

Only you and I can know
    The nights we struggled through,
With you hanging on for me,
    And me hanging on for you.

Sometimes our sense of humor
    Was all that got us by.
We learned that the more we laughed
    The less time we had to cry.

So I think of all the happiness
    Each day can hold in store,
And I wish them all for you, Mom,
    'Cause no one deserves it more.

Written by Buffy for her mother

* * * * *

Lorraine and Bill minister through singing southern Gospel and their testimonies out of Brookfield, OH and can be reached at 330-448-7734.

Sweet Inspirations

Marsha Kamovitch

In 1991 I felt such a grieving emptiness inside. I'd gone to church all my life, but I had no idea what it meant to be "born again."

This emptiness caused me to read books and I began to watch the 700 Club. I'd never even had a desire to read the Bible, but I began to hunger for something more in my life to fill this strange void in me, so one day I asked Jesus to come into my heart - and He did!

My brother-in-law, Frank Kamovitch, had been coaxing me to go to Crossing Paths Ministry's Bible study on Tuesday nights; so I went. Having fellowship with other Christians and learning more of God's Word there helped me grow in my Christian walk.

My life changed drastically. What was even more wonderful was that I saw my husband Rich begin to do things differently. Although he never said anything about having commitment to Jesus, he started to read the Bible with me and watch Christian TV - something was different

We'd never had marriage problems. When I became the young bride of Richard Kamovitch, we had great plans for the future. Rich said, "I'm going to make enough money to retire in my forties so we can have fun." "Fun" to Rich and I then was going to the mountains, snowmobiling, running off to car races, watching the Steelers, and partying. Rich was driving a truck selling tools to garages when we were first married, but he began to see the potential of having his own company. Amazingly he made enough money to retire and have his "dream."

Yet in 1991 when that fast-paced life style didn't fill my needs, evidently it didn't fill Rich's either. He finally admitted to me that he'd made Jesus Lord of his life. At first he refused to go with me to dinners and study groups. He went to a picnic, and after that we went together. Such a blessed time for both of us. His appetite for booze, vulgar movies, the things he'd always done, became less and less.

On Good Friday of 1995 my husband began to act differently. He didn't say anything, but I knew something special had taken place. After two days he finally said "I've got something to tell you." Then he told me of his experience. "I was praying, and suddenly it felt as though electricity went through me and I lit up like a light bulb. "I knew something happened," I told him. He asked me, "How did you know?" I could see it in your face." I could have told him he was shining like a light bulb! No doubt existed in Rich's or my mind - he'd had a close encounter with Jesus. The bond between us grew stronger.

But Rich began to have acute stomach pain. He grew pale and thin. His face looked pale and sickly. We went to doctor after doctor, seeking the reason for his physical problems.

On August 3 we heard the medical diagnosis, "You have terminal pancreatic cancer." The doctor took me aside to say, "He has two months to live."

WOW! What do you do when you're hit with such a bomb? We prayed. Everyone prayed. Rich and I read the Bible three times a day. During his illness he had one desire - to serve the Lord. Before he died, he totally abandoned himself to Jesus.

The two of us had a bond like we never had before. Rich even appeared on TV saying, "I'm in a win-win situation." If

I die, I'll be with Jesus; if I live, I'll serve him."

Rich's medical prognosis was that he'd live just two months; he lived ten! He died on May 30, 1996. At his funeral he appeared on TV - telling his friends and relatives that they needed to come to Jesus! His appearance on screen caught everyone's attention.

Needless to say, my grief has been difficult. If ever I needed to lean on Jesus, it has been since my beloved husband's death. In Isaiah 54 the Lord tells how He can be my Comforter, during my time of grieving. Even though he physically died, I KNOW Rich is in heaven with Jesus.

Two weeks after his death, something woke me up. Looking up at the ceiling, I saw an angel hovering. Closing my eyes, I wondered if I were hallucinating. Yet when I opened them, the angel was still there and stayed for awhile. I'd had a difficult time sleeping before that, but I had no trouble after that. I slept like a contented infant. Rich was missing, but the angel assured me that the Lord was there.

In the weeks that followed, God gave me a gift. Time after time I'd awaken, and I'd begin to write poems - such a strange phenomenon when all my life I'd hated to even write a letter.

On September 5 my bedroom was totally dark when I went to sleep, but then I awoke and found the room was lit up with a brilliant light. An angel stood at the foot of my bed. It looked like a girl angel who reminded me of myself the night Rich and I went to our high school prom. She stayed for awhile, but then she was gone. The Lord inspired me then to write another poem, "Angel Mine." I wrote but then the words ceased to flow. "Lord," I prayed, "please help me finish this poem. I'm tired and want to go to bed."

After my prayer the ending came and again I slept, feeling His love and comfort.

"Angel Mine"

The Lord has sent you from above,
To this earth as like a dove.
His assignment, you carry through,
For one that He had given to you.
Angel mine, you came to me,
God's good gift, to set me free.
You spoke no words, but let me know,
You've been sent by God and then you go.
Into my room you gently crept,
For this is where we always met.
As I slept, you gently stirred,
I bolted and looked, my eyes still blurred.
Unexpectedly, I gave a shout,
A moment later you were out.
You gave a glimpse of eternal life,
To let me know everything's all right.
Angel mine, you've been sent to me,
To calm the oceans of my seas.
Gentle spirit, from above,
You shared with me our Savior's love.

My grief has also been helped by helping others. By helping them, I have found I help myself. Involvement in the Christian fellowship and with my church through its Bereavement Support Group has opened doors for me to share Christ's love. More than that, my poems have been put together in a book called "Sweet Inspirations" which many have claimed has helped their grieving spirits to know that, regardless of their circumstances, Jesus is there and He Cares.

* * * * *

You may purchase "Sweet Inspirations" by contacting Son-Rise Publications, 143 Greenfield Road, New Wilmington, PA 16142 or by phone 1-800-358-0777.

The Transformation

Woody Young

Imagine my parents horror when I fell on the playground and hit my head against a drain pipe; splitting it open and severing the nerve endings to the right side of my brain. I'd started out the day as an over exuberant 18-month-old handful, but suddenly I was a handicapped toddler.

The severity of the blow had hindered my speech and coordination so severely that I really couldn't talk until I was five years old. Even then I had a terrible speech impediment -- stuttering and slurring my words.

My father and mother were afraid to leave me alone so they put my older sister Shirlee in charge of me. Injury prone, I had more bruises and bumps in the next five years than most people do in a lifetime. You would have thought I'd played some dangerous sport looking at my many scars and broken bones. After contemplating the past, I sometimes wonder how much overtime my guardian angels had to work.

Imagine my humiliation when the kids at my elementary school teased and tormented me. When they would choose sides for a game, of course, nobody wanted me on their team. To make matters worse, they were never nice about it.

Because of all the humiliation I experienced, my insecurities caused me to console myself by eating. When I grew as wide as I was tall, they had more reasons to poke fun at me with another nickname, "Fatty."

Because of my handicaps the church became very special to me. The teacher said what I wanted to hear - "Jesus loves you." Everyone at church seemed to have compassion, even the kids. It seemed to me that I received more consideration there than anywhere else. To me the church is so much more than a building. It is people who reach out to love and to care. I wanted to be kind and considerate to them because they were so kind to me, but I had little desire to reach out with love to anyone outside the church.

Reading, spelling, and punctuation, all eluded me. By the time I went to high school, I was a functional illiterate in grammatical skills. In the eleventh grade I wrote a letter to the school newspaper and signed it "An unhappy eleventh grader." My English teacher used my epistle for an example and tore it apart for spelling, grammar, and punctuation. Even though I had not signed it, I still felt that everyone in the class knew that I was the author. My face burned with embarrassment as she declared that the writer had no right to be in the eleventh grade. As I squirmed in my seat, a voice inside my head said, "If you don't want to be embarrassed, don't ever write again." That message would repeat over and over again every time I attempted to write and would keep me from putting my feelings in print for years to come.

As time passed I was able to read and write better. I even managed to graduate from college, get married, and have two beautiful daughters as well as a successful business. All this happened despite my insecurities and the years it took to overcome my handicaps.

I grew in wisdom and my stature improved (I lost all those excess pounds) and found favor with God and man. As I was scanning the Bible one day in 1984, I felt a nudging from the Lord, "It's time for you to read the Bible."

I protested, "I already do that."

His reply? "You read it like a snack or a fast food." At that point I felt as though He was saying, "You sift through Matthew, Mark, Luke, and John, but you've never read My Word from cover to cover."

Even though I have attended church all my life, I had to admit I had not read the Bible cover to cover. I realized I needed to do that and committed right then to read the Bible beginning to end.

In one year I fulfilled the promise which totally changed my life. I didn't go through the Sacred Word as a devotional, but I savored what God's messages had to say.

When I realized I didn't understand all the passages, I went back and read the entire Book again. I have read it cover to cover many times since. I get so engrossed at times that my wife, Beth, says, "Hey, don't you need to go to work?" I do, but thankfully I work for my own company, and the boss doesn't object if I'm late!

But I have a far greater Employer who I now choose to love and to serve. For 40 years I had known about Jesus, but as I delved into His Word, He became my Best Friend. I came to understand the Scripture which says, *"Ye must be born again."* I knew from my new relationship with Him that I had moved my head knowledge from my head to my heart.

He started to work in my life in such a way that I was literally transformed. My family, my customers, my vendors, all claimed they could see a difference. My physical change is not as apparent as the spiritual change that came about when I was reborn into God's Kingdom.

Imagine my amazement when I went to a conference, and a woman prophesied that I was going to become a great writer. At first I scoffed at the idea, remembering the years of burning tears, and the humiliation I'd experienced when I wrote the letter in the eleventh grade. The still, small voice reminded me once more that if I wrote anything of substance, that I'd be held up in ridicule again.

Yet a nagging persisted within me to put down on paper the things I have learned from the Lord over the years. To my amazement, I found the Holy Spirit took over my thoughts and my words as I wrote! I am living proof that when King Jesus transforms a life, He does it completely. I've authored many books - me, the least likely to write anything. All the credit goes to the Lord. Of course, success requires more than just believing. I had to put my faith into action.

In a book that I was privileged to coauthor with Chuck Missler, we shared about the Second Coming which we both believe will happen soon. One of the true joys in my life is reading the many letters from readers whose lives have been touched by something I have written. Like this one - "My name is Michael, I am currently in prison. I have just read your book <u>Countdown to Eternity</u> and must say that it has given me more understanding than anything I have ever read about the Bible. I am interested in getting Volume II as soon as it is released. Thank you very much for the priceless information you have already shared with me. May God bless you and your efforts."

Serving the Lord has made my life exciting! I have great joy, so much so that I've had the blessing of sharing God's Word and its meaning through my publishing company with that name. - Joy Publishing.

All of this has happened to the youngster who had many physical and emotional problems. The Lord truly is in the transformation business. If He can give me such a rewarding life in spite of my earlier handicaps, just imagine what He can do for you! Seek Him above all things, and you shall receive the desires of your heart. For the Lord truly cares for you!

* * * * *

Woody Young can be reached at Joy Publishing, P.O. Box 9901, Fountain Valley, CA 92708.

Following his huge success on Countdown I, he is planning to publish Countdown II in 1999.

His website www.joypublishing.com.

New Kidney, New Heart, New Start

Ken Salzwimmer

At three in the morning pain and sickness brought me out of my sleep. My bride of four days lay beside me.

I had taken ill earlier on the Wednesday prior to our wedding. My right foot had started to swell then, but I'd attributed that to a sled riding incident I'd had with the kids from my youth group. The doctors couldn't see anything wrong when they examined and x-rayed my foot; but putting the considerable pain and misery aside, I'd borrowed a friend's larger shoes, and as a younger-than-average groom, I hobbled down the aisle with a cane. Some start for a marriage!

However, that middle-of-the-night illness was definitely NOT from an accident. I writhed from pain and sickness all over.

The next thing I knew I was being poked and prodded by doctors. One finally asked me, "Are you my new kidney patient?"

My first clue! Up until that moment I had no idea what was wrong with me.

Some other words I heard were not encouraging ones for a new husband to hear, "By all rights, you should be dead."

All I could do then was rely on The Source that I'd been

so close to most of my life - Jesus. Because of Him I had gone into the youth ministry. I knew He could perform miracles; I also knew He used doctors to heal.

I remember a shunt being put in and needles piercing me. The next thing I knew, I was hooked up to this machine for survival.

Every Tuesday, Thursday, and Saturday I had to get up from bed at four in the morning and prepare myself for 3½ hours of sitting in a chair while hooked up to this strange dialysis machine. I tell my kids at church the best way I can explain it is to say that it's a washing machine to wash and clean my blood; but I also knew that during the process, it was also taking out some of the good. Resentment built up in me because of the fifteen hours that I had to spend every week on the dialysis machine, so much that I began to pray that my turn would come to receive a new kidney. Every time I inquired about my prospects, I heard such comments as, "Ken, you're not sick enough."

How sick did I need to be? I prayed and waited. And waited. No promises came my way, so I began to wonder if I was going to live and die as a slave to the dialysis machine. Besides, things were taking place in my body that made me aware it was breaking down.

On September 3, 1998, I met with Pastor Willoughby at the "Golden Arches." While working on a project, we were startled as the door burst open and Susan, the pastor's wife came in. "Ken," she said breathlessly, "the transplant office is trying to reach you."

Her words had no impact at first because I was thinking of the Dialysis Center, and this didn't sound good to me.

Earlier in the year I felt the Lord had indicated that I was going to have another hospital experience very soon. When the word "transplant" finally hit, we ran off to my van. Using my cell phone, I dialed. Boy, was I shaky! For 3½ years I'd been waiting, and I thought I'd never hear those words. My heart sang as "Bertie," a coordinator, answered the phone.

"Ken, you're third in line for a kidney and yours is a perfect match."

At 3:45 that afternoon the roller coaster ride began - up and down - rushing, following orders. On top of everything else, I had to find a dentist after hours to extract a problem tooth just in case it was abscessed. No infections dared be in my body at the time of surgery.

At 8:30 that evening the green light came - GO! Off to the hospital one more time — but I didn't mind that trip.

About 7:45 the next morning I received my new kidney. "Thank You, Jesus! New kidney, new heart, new start!"

During my two-week stay in the hospital, God brought me through a new, spiritual, life-changing experience. No earthly words can explain the depth of the love God revealed to me then. His words poured out, "I love you, my son! You are mine. I want to talk to you." Those words were very clear that first day.

The staff took two days to find a Bible. After that the Lord began to reveal His heart-filled words of the Psalms. He started with this experience!

The day my new kidney woke up finally came. Just a few days before this the doctor had explained to me that my new kidney was sleeping and that it could wake up in a few days, weeks, or even months. How I praised the Lord the next morning when the doctor walked in and greeted me with, "She's awake and doing great!"

After he left the room, tears began to fill my eyes; and I prayed with great thanksgiving to my Heavenly Father for all the many blessings on my life.

Then He took me into His heart-felt pages to Psalms 139. This Psalm had been my lifetime favorite. Many years ago while I served as a Scout Chaplain, I had prayed for a lifetime Word from the Lord. I have preached that Psalm to thousands of scouts all around the country and hope that you will prayerfully study it also.

He then led me to read verse 13. *"For you created my innermost being; you knit me together in my Mother's womb."*

verse 14: *"I praise you because I am fearfully and wonderfully made."* verse 15: *"My frame was not hidden from you when I was made in the secret place. When I was woven together in the depths of the earth."* verse 16: *"Your eyes saw my unformed body. All the days ordained for me were written in your book before one of them came to be."* I saw God's Word in a new light, and I was thirsting for knowledge as I continued to read verse after verse.

The wonderment of *"He knew me before I was even conceived"* made me cry as I was thinking of my new kidney and how God had known that a kidney would be available for me even yet before I was conceived! I just started praising Jesus!

After that truly heavenly encounter, verses 17 and 18 in the Living Bible took on a whole new meaning for me. I thought how precious it is to realize that God is thinking about me constantly! I can't count the times each day when I know God's thoughts turn toward me or when I awaken in the morning and feel His presence. Many a morning I would awaken and immediately feel His loving arms wrapped around me and know that He had been watching over me through the night.

As God continued to give me scripture, I just rejoiced in the knowledge He was imparting. He led me on to verse 23, *"Search me, O God and know my heart."* Let this be our prayer together. Let us come to a place where we truly mean those words and then be willing to be broken of one's self. We must be broken of self because when God does the searching, He will also be revealing to us the deep, inner parts of our heart. We must be willing to listen. It is in our minds that Satan will attempt to have us fight battles that have already been won at the cross. We must resist and pray that our Heavenly Father will show us His thoughts, His way, and His will!

We all must pray every day and ask for God's wisdom in what we are doing before we do it!

As God kept revealing to me His love, He led me to the

book of Proverbs, where He says in Chapter 8, verse 11, *"My son, do not despise the Lord's discipline, do not reject His rebuke, because the Lord disciplines those He loves."* Then I knew in my heart that my road wasn't going to be easy.

Verse 13 says, *"Blessed is the man who finds wisdom, and the man who gains understanding."* How often I'd spoken without praying for an answer. I cried out to the Lord, *"Fill me with your wisdom."* Through my tears He took me into Chapter 3 of Proverbs. Pray with me for the Lord's discipline. Do not resent His rebuke for He chastens those He loves and His message is also for the church. Read Proverbs and ask the Lord to open your heart.

After reading verse 19, *"By Wisdom the Lord laid the earth's foundation, by understanding He set the heavens in place,"* I felt that heaven had come down into my hospital room. In verse 20, *"By His knowledge the deeps were divided, and the clouds let drop the dew."* The Lord spoke to me that day in verse 21 which I liken to a bright light. *"My son, preserve sound judgment and discernment, do not let them out of your sight!"*

I said, "Yes, Lord, yes!" Verse 22, *"They will be life for you, an ornament to grace your neck."* Verse 23, *"Then you will go on your way in safety and your foot will not stumble."*

More of God's Wisdom came before my eyes in verse 24 *"For she is more profitable than silver and yields better returns than gold, she is more precious than rubies; nothing you desire can compare with her."*

When I read *"silver and gold,"* God spoke. Again in tears, I knew this was going to be like one of those bitter pills to take. The Lord reminded me this was also for the church. Silver and gold things, credit cards, spending — how easy it is for me to like things for us at Christmas. We need to be very careful of what we want. We need to seek God's Wisdom - do you really need those things? How much have we spent on things which we could have done without and could have given to ministries, missions, the needy, widows, or poor children? All I had began thinking about was what I could do after I got home. How can I give to others - my time, my all, and my money, which is the Lord's anyway. I want to give even more of myself to others. I want to reach lost souls, for our time is not long to reach them.

In the hospital, the Lord drew me into prayer. Different people's names would come to me. I prayed and reached Heaven. I prayed for the people in our church that have much the same needs.

God showed me how easy it is to fall for Satan's snare, for today the god of this world is things - yes, it is a material world. Many Christians today work SO hard and SO often and spend SO much for things. These are the words the Lord shared with me. I felt that a long time ago I gave up my collection of 500 ceramic green frogs and I did!

I have learned so much from my hospital experience. The words from my heart were, "Yes, Lord, Yes!" Each time it seemed like heaven came even nearer.

You yourself must have your own experience as you open God's love-filled pages. I know He will speak to you just as He has started on me.

I now know why it took me longer to get out of the hospital, and in some ways I didn't want to leave there. I can't tell you everything in only a few pages. I have so much more to share — many things just written down on paper towels. I felt His love for me in the most disciplining of my life, and all I wanted to say was, "Yes, Lord, yes, Lord!"

I have learned and grown from my hospital experience as He came over and over saying, "Ken, I want to talk to you and remind you that this is for you and the church." I ask you again to be open to God's Word for yourself as I share another day of my encounter with my Heavenly Father.

As I opened His Word again, He started out as a Father to me, His son. *"Listen, my son, to a Father's instructions,"* Chapter 4 of Proverbs, verse 1. Many times from my heart those words were repeated, *"Listen, my son, pay attention and gain understanding."* In verse 2, *"I give you sound learn-*

ing, so do not forsake my teaching." In verse 4, He taught me and said, *"Lay hold of my words with all your heart. Keep my commands and you will live."*

I couldn't get away from the words at the start. In Chapter 4, verse 1 of Proverbs, *"Listen, my son, to your Father's instructions."* My mind went back to times when I had to put something together and would open the box and put aside the paper which said "Instructions." I likened it to another story. A little boy comes running into the living room. As he passes by his father, he says "Dad, look at my new model car kit." The father replied, "Do you want my help?" As the son dumps the box of parts onto the living room floor, he answered back to his father, "No! I can do it myself." By this time he had all the parts out of the box, and he put aside the paper saying those words, "Instructions" which had been enclosed in the box.

The son worked hard and long. The father heard his son's cry, "It is finished! I did it myself!" He then went over to his father, carrying in both his hands his finished model car. The son placed his model car onto the floor and said again, "Look at what I have done all by myself!" Then he started to push the model car across the floor, and it all fell apart.

The wise father came over with a smile on his face and said, "Now, my son, let me help you. First of all we WILL start with the instructions." A little while later, with the father and son working together, the model car kit was finished. How happy the son was as again he pushed the model car across the floor, and it stayed together. How happy both the father and son were for they had followed the instructions.

We may not think or say it, and many times don't even know that we are doing what the little boy had done — gone ahead in our own strength and our own experience without even going to the Heavenly Father for wisdom and instructions in prayer. We just must say, "we," or "I, did it myself!" I know one thing for sure, the Heavenly Father would not be pleased.

In verse 4, He said, *"Lay hold of my words with all your heart."* I've found it to be true that no matter what Christian job you do, if you do it from the head, you may do it well, but before long you'll find yourself tired and worn out and the ministry becomes old to you. That's why many Christians burn out and quit. But when you lay hold with all your heart, the first thing you want to do is go before your Heavenly Father in prayer and ask for instructions. All the while you do your task from the heart, you are always wanting to know His Will, and you always want to please the Heavenly Father.

Back to verse 4, *"Keep my commands and you will live."* Verse 5, *"Get Wisdom, get understanding, do not forget my words or swerve from them."*

Verse 10 says, *"Listen, my son, accept what I say, and the years of your life will be many."* Verse 11, *"I guide you in the way of Wisdom, and lead you along straight paths."* Verse 12, *"When you walk, your steps will not be hampered; when you run, you will not stumble."* Verse 13, *"Hold onto instructions, do not let it go! Guard it well, for it is your life."*

After two weeks, I honestly regretted leaving my hospital room. Those intimate times with Jesus will always remain deep in my heart, but I knew He wanted me to pass His message on to each of you because He loves YOU, too!

For we Christians need to stop passing by the Heavenly Father's instructions, but stop dead in our tracks and listen for His Wisdom and find out what is God's will for us at this time. We will gain His understanding, His sound learning, and His teaching. Keep His commands and the church will really come alive and live.

For this again came to me from my hospital experience, and He reminded me it's for the church today.

Well, that has been just another day before my Heavenly Father, and I replied "Yes, Lord, yes, to Your will and Your way." There is still a lot to share from the new theme of my life, "New Kidney, New Heart, New Start!"

* * * * *

Pastor Salzwimmer can be reached in Hubbard, OH by calling 330-534-1265.

When Life Throws You A Curve

Tom McGough

If I were to have the opportunity to condense my life story into one thought, it would be that out of life's greatest trials can come God's greatest blessings when we learn to become wholly dependent on Him. Romans 8:28 captures this promise so well: *"And we know that all things work together for good to those that love the Lord."*

I was five years old when I got involved in baseball. I think probably that at first I was mimicking my older brothers. I would go to their Little League games, and it looked like something I wanted to be involved in. At five years of age I decided that I wanted to be a ball player. And not just any ball player. I wanted to pitch with the Pittsburgh Pirates.

My father kept me equipped with Wilson Indestructo baseballs, and my ball field, for the most part, was a parking lot and the side of a shopping center. I used to throw balls off the wall. I threw my first baseball against the wall so many times that I was able to wear the cover off of it. When I got a little older, Little League age, I started to throw pretty hard. I threw it so hard that cracks would develop in the baseball. And then, at the last stage, when I was in high school, I used to throw the ball so hard that eventually the ball would actually crack in half.

I remember so vividly the fall of my senior year in high school. 1972. I was invited to a workout down at Three Rivers Stadium. I remember going there with my mom and dad. There were baseball bats as the handles to the doors as you walked into the Pirate front office. I was just so excited, just thinking, "Mom and Dad, this is what we've worked for. This is the dream." I had a uniform, went out onto the field, and got to work out. I started to throw and I was just so excited, working on pure adrenaline. Harding Peterson, the scouting supervisor, said, "Are you ready to cut one loose?" Well, Dave Ricketts was the bullpen catcher, and he didn't have any equipment on. I guess he looked at me and figured, "How hard can this kid throw? He's in high school. He's seventeen years old." Well, my first pitch came in at close to 100 miles an hour. His eyes got real big. In a joking gesture, he went back in, and he got two of every type of equipment that a catcher would wear. Roberto Clemente, who was perched on the bullpen fence, nearly fell off the fence laughing at Dave's over-reaction.

Everything progressed nicely. I pitched four games the next spring, my senior year in high school. It started out with one scout from the Los Angeles Dodgers for my first game. At my second ball game there were about a dozen; at the third ball game, about 25. The fourth and final game that I pitched, about 50 scouts, representing all of the different major league teams, were there - scouting directors, farm directors, head of minor league systems, even general managers in some instances.

And I remember the night before the draft, June 4, 1973, getting several calls from different teams just saying that the draft is very unpredictable. "We have no idea if we're going to be able to get you or not, but you're on the top of our list for the northeast, the top player we scouted." So I really believed at that point that I would have the opportunity to play professional ball.

The next day, at 5 o'clock in the afternoon after the news blackout was lifted, I got a call from Dennis Lustig of the

Cleveland Plain Dealer. "Tommy," he said, "I'm calling to let you know that you have been chosen as Cleveland's first pitcher choice in the Summer Free Agent Draft today in New York City. What are your thoughts?"

I was speechless. It was just absolutely incredible.

I had little helmets aligned on the desk. The way I would signal my parents what team I was drafted by would be to reach down and take the appropriate helmet and clip it to my key chain while I was still on the phone. I remember so vividly, reaching down and grabbing the Cleveland helmet, clipping it onto my key chain, and just having such a rush of emotion. This was something that I'd worked so hard for, something that I'd dreamed about for three quarters of my life. And now God was allowing it to come to fruition.

But the real major league story was how I came to know Jesus Christ.

I went through the minor league system, being probably the top pitcher in the Gulf Coast Rookie League. I was getting a lot of accolades, getting a lot of attention, but again it all was just fueling this feeling of self-righteousness.

Now, let me set the stage for you.

I was born and raised in a Christian home, attended a Bible-believing, Spirit-led church. My mom and dad really lived the Christian walk, really taught by example. But it wasn't until I went away, out of high school and into professional baseball, that I was challenged.

When I came home the off-season of 1975-76, I was challenged by what were referred to then as "Jesus freaks." These were people who God had pulled from hell, literally. Kids that had been involved in drugs, kids that had been thrown out of school for disobedience or just bad behavior. These were kids that the world found real easy to judge. They still had outward signs of worldliness, still had a look about them as though they were rebellious. But, deep down inside, God had taken out their stone hearts of sin and replaced them with new hearts of love.

I can remember half a dozen incidents where these folks

would come up to me and say, "You know, brother, it's not by works of righteousness that one is saved, but it's by the grace of God."

I would get very irritated and would think to myself, "How dare you tell me how to get right with God? I'm a good kid. I've made good conscious decisions. I've decided not to get involved with drugs. I've decided not to be a womanizer."

My mother would read Bible stories to me. I've had memory verses, catechism; I was baptized; I was active in my church youth group in high school. I had all of the credentials one could have. When I signed, I tithed what I received as a bonus to the church and to God's work.

But I had a barrier that was much worse. I had a barrier of self-righteousness. I knew of the miracle of Easter. I knew of the miracle of Christ's birth, Emmanuel, God with us. But I thought of grace as being something that was good for somebody else, not me. "Hey," I thought, "if you've made bad decisions, if you've made a wreck of your life, okay, fine, then you need grace. But I haven't made those same bad decisions. I've consciously walked the good walk. I've consciously done the right things."

I had all of the right moves but with the wrong motivation. It was Tom McGough doing it and not the Spirit of God through me.

And so, this particular off season, I was challenged. I was convinced they were wrong. I was convinced that, for every verse they were quoting, that there would be a counter verse that would say that you had to do this, that you had to do that, thou shalt this, thou shalt that. I was convinced that it was there.

I went to spring training the next year believing that I was going to be able to justify the unjustifiable, that I was going to find those verses that would justify my position of works, that I was going to work my way into heaven. As I read through the New Testament, I just couldn't believe my eyes. Every passage I was reading reinforced that it is the grace of God, not works. One of the first verses that really struck home with me was Ephesians 2:8 and 9. *"For by grace are ye saved through faith and that not of yourselves, it is the gift of God, not of works, lest any man should boast."*

At the end of spring training I met a fella, Glenn Redman, who had just been released by the San Francisco Giants. I truly believe he tried to hook up with another team simply to witness to some of the young players like me. The first time I met Glenn, I held out my hand to shake his hand, I looked him straight in the eyes, and I said, "Glenn, it's a pleasure to meet you." And, without so much as a stutter, he looked right back at me and he said, "God has a plan for your life." I thought to myself, "These Christians, they're everywhere. I can't lose these people!" But God's message was persistent and consistent. He wanted me to know the truth that, unlike baseball where my hard work would be rewarded, I couldn't work my way into heaven. I couldn't be good enough. I couldn't do enough good things. "All have sinned and fallen short of the glory of God, none are righteous, no not one." At that point Glenn and I had many conversations, and at that point I accepted Jesus Christ into my life. I received the baptism in the Holy Spirit and I am a changed man. I will tell you, what you see in me now is no longer me, but what you see is charismata, the power of God that enables.

After I made that commitment to Jesus Christ, He blessed me wonderfully in baseball, later in business, and in my family with my wonderful wife Luci and our two boys Eric and Scott. But my faith hadn't yet been put to the test.

In 1992 I took a major step in faith. My business wasn't fitting in with the needs of my life at that time. I was out of town a lot, and my boys needed me at home. So, at the age of 37, I left business and went to an entry-level position at WPIT-FM in Pittsburgh. There I started a radio program - "Street Level." One of the things that gave me a sense of security with that station was that it had been broadcasting in the same format since 1947. But nine months later, in January of '93, WPIT went off the air. I felt like the rug had been pulled out from under me. I woke up the next morning wondering, "What am I going to do, I'm the sole bread winner?"

I went to WAVL in Apollo, Pennsylvania, to find an outlet for "Street Level." When I asked station manager, Bob Dain, if he could use a 15-minute program, he said that Luis Palau had just cancelled, and he was looking for a 15-minute program. God opened the opportunity for "Street Level" to get on the air, but also for me to get a part-time job.

That summer God provided for our every need. In June we needed tires that cost $83. Luci got out the summer clothes from the attic, put her hand in a pocket, and there was the $83 for the tires. We found stock we never knew we had purchased. God provided free tickets so that we were able to take the boys to Waldemere Park on Lake Erie. In business I had made a lot of phone calls. That summer Luci found some certificates for free nights at a nice hotel that we'd received as a result, so we were able to take the boys to Niagara Falls.

A long time ago I promised God that I would never take an honorarium for speaking, but sometimes churches will send me checks anyway. We've always voided them and returned them. That summer we had several hundred dollars in honorarium checks. I asked Luci, "Do you think this is God's way of providing for us?"

She said, "How many times have you said that crisis doesn't change the promise?" So I voided the checks and sent them back posthaste!

God was so faithful. The experience really gave depth to my faith. This was a real growing point. I had no choice but to believe God just as the Israelites had no choice when they faced the Red Sea in front of them and Pharaoh's army approaching from behind.

In August of 1993 the doors opened at Cornerstone TeleVision. What a blessing. In fact, if someone had asked me five years earlier, if they'd said, "Just for fun, what would be the best job in the world?" I could never have imagined being the host of "SportsWeek," a nationally syndicated television sports program. "SportsWeek" is the perfect culmination of every job experience God has allowed me to have, utilizing the skills that He developed in me from my baseball training, business training, and on-air training in radio.

Perhaps it would be foolish for someone to say that they enjoyed those inevitable times of testing in life, but I have certainly come to look at difficult circumstances differently. It is only through the fire that we can be purified, and each period of testing in my life has merely been a prelude to a period of uncommon blessing from God.

So, if you are in the midst of one of those extremely difficult times in your life, take heart! As you draw closer to God, He is simply preparing you to be able to receive His uncommon blessing.

Story as told to: Jean Stewart

* * * * *

Tom McGough is still hosting "SportsWeek" on Cornerstone Television, Wall, PA.

Renewed Commitment

Charlene Borsic-Pasko

Mom and Dad provided well for us. I never was deprived of anything, but somehow I never felt as though I measured up to what my mother expected of me. I found out later that Mom was always proud of my accomplishments, but she never told ME about her feelings then. She told other people of the things she thought I did right. I danced a little and did various teenage activities. At school I never was great at academics, but I realize now that it was because I never really applied myself.

Yet the Lord has been good to me. At age twenty I captured my young life's dream. United Airlines accepted me and I became a flight attendant. I started flying across the United States and was based in Miami, Florida. Later in my career I flew all over the world.

At twenty-three Florida provided great times, and lots of boyfriends. I thought I had everything going for me until one day I realized I had an emptiness inside. I hadn't been attending church at the time. I remember telling one of my roommates, "This empty, empty feeling comes over me. I have no idea how to fill it up." Little did I understand then that the Holy Spirit was wooing me.

I never got into the drug or drinking scene even though everyone around me was "doing it" in the late 60's and early 70's. Thank heaven I never had an urge to try out either drugs or alcohol. That just never happened.

However, men always seemed to be attracted to me, but I never quite got the recognition I craved from my father. He passed away fifteen or sixteen years ago. My mother has told me how much Dad loved me, but I never felt the closeness, the oneness with him that I wanted.

My two brothers were five and three years older and I was the baby. I was basically left alone a lot in the house to do my own thing. My mom was doing her golfing, bingo or bowling. She'd have someone come over, a girl friend or whatever, but at 6:00 my mom was out of the house doing something. Part of the reason she did this was because she didn't get to do a lot of things while she was growing up.

In giving this testimony, there are things that I'm holding back because I don't want to offend any of my family members. But there were some hardships we endured and some quiet secrets that ended up being a part of my life and that caused me to not go forth with lasting relationships. I had many different romances as a young woman. I was never without someone asking me out. I didn't have a problem with that area. I attracted some good men but ended up with a few bad ones too. Some were abusive, mostly verbal. I was really never physically abused, although one young man tried to choke me when I was in my early-to-mid thirties. Once I was nearly raped. Looking back, it seems that Satan was trying to get me at my weakest place — men. I had thought that if I could just find the right man to make me happy, that all this would go away.

But it never did. I tried marriage, but failed. When I was expecting my second child, my marriage went sour because my husband had an affair with the babysitter. I was 28 and my oldest son was two. I was still flying at the time, but was off on leave. My life had reached the desperation point. I didn't think I was going to make it. Now I realize that a lot of the things that happened were not just one person's fault — it takes both partners to make a problem.

When I married, my husband and I were unequally yoked in Jesus. I had not continued to walk with the Lord.

Although at 23 when I had had that empty feeling I mentioned, I had accepted Jesus into my heart and made Him my Savior. But I didn't make Him my Lord. I didn't have the teaching or role models of what a Christian should be; so I ended up marrying someone who was not a Christian, and I wasn't living as a follower of Jesus should.

Years before, I was baptized in the Holy Spirit in my bedroom, back in my home in Warren, Ohio, where my parents lived, with no understanding of what was taking place. The Holy Spirit had baptized me. I spoke in tongues. I had called my cousins, Eric and Grace Wilson, both of whom are still very close to me today, and told them what had happened. They said, "God loves you very much and He is giving you a gift." They explained what speaking in tongues was all about. I even looked it up in scriptures, but I still didn't grow in my faith. I used my prayer language once in a while, but I got right back into the world of flying and meeting people. So when I got married and was unequally yoked with my partner and I wasn't walking with Jesus Christ, the marriage didn't work out.

Giving birth to my second child was a tremendous testimony of Jesus' love. When Eric and Grace stopped over, my time was close. About two weeks before my due date, they came into my house and said, "We want to lay hands on you so that when you go for your delivery, you will have a totally easy time." They prayed, then left. Several hours later my mother appeared at my door out of nowhere and said, "You know, Charlene, I think I'm going to spend the night with you. It seems like a mother's love is needed at a time like this." Jesus' proved His love is needed even more.

We headed to bed. My two-year-old little Wayne was in his bed when I went to mine. My husband was gone. Since he began his affair, he had been removed from the house at my request because of all the stress I was going through. I ended up going to the hospital in the middle of the night, so Mom had to call my girlfriend Kathy to come and stay with Wayne. When we arrived at St. Joe's Hospital which was about three blocks away, I was ready to deliver and had very little pain.

One nurse checked me and asked, "How long have you been in labor?"

"Not very long," I replied.

She told me not to do anything until Dr. Milheim came in. When he arrived, he said, "Char, you sure didn't waste any time!"

Off we went to the delivery room. When I began to give birth, I suddenly felt completely, hopelessly alone. My mom had driven me there but was still signing me into the hospital and hadn't made it upstairs. No husband, no moral support. I became wrapped in a cocoon of self pity. Could this really be happening to me? Lord, I've made so many mistakes! All this turmoil was going through my head.

I'd been blaming myself for so many things, but at that moment of birth I felt Jesus' abundant love for me. Without even speaking to Him or hearing an audible voice—it was more like a soul-to-soul anointing of Jesus' love—I heard Him asking, "Charlene, what is your love for Me?" I could not even think of anything else but the tremendous flood of love that began encompassing me.

I said to Him without words, "Jesus, Lord God, I love You more than anything in this world." At that same time, I was actually giving birth to my new son, Eric. I embraced all of the love Jesus was giving me, and I felt as if I was going toward Him, almost like in a cloud. I didn't see any white lights or anything, but I felt this love and I wanted to be there with Him. It didn't matter that I was giving birth, and I didn't feel any love greater than His. After my second baby was born, I was so excited about what God had done in that split-second which had seemed like an eternity of love. After I pushed my son out and the doctor was stitching me, I sat up partially and said, "I had a visit from the Lord and He wished me happiness!"

I kept repeating that statement over and over right then in St. Joe's Catholic Hospital. To my right stood a nun. To my left was a dark-haired lady labor nurse. Beside her stood my doctor who was Jewish (which I didn't think about until later when God revealed this to me).

At the point when I'd felt so utterly alone, God had revealed His love and asked me how I felt. I knew He wanted an answer. I had to give an answer. I could see those around me viewed my experience with skepticism as I shared what had gone on as best I could.

The older nun said, "You're just not thinking right. You're delirious."

The lady nurse at my left didn't say a thing, but my doctor grabbed my toes and said, "I believe you, Charlene, I believe you!" They were cleaning up Eric before I ever asked if my new baby was a boy or girl because Jesus had visited me and had given me this great feeling of love. When they laid little Eric in my arms, I was so joyful and I bathed him in love. I could have said something more about my visit from the Lord, but I began to realize that I couldn't explain what had taken place. I kept silent after that.

The nurse visited me later and said that what I had told them had taken place had never happened before that she knew of. She said, "I've been working here for sixteen years and have never heard of such an experience." She told me, "Don't ever let anyone take that wonderful happening away from you." She went on to say, "I've been an atheist all my life, but your experience has changed my thinking."

Being raised a Catholic, I have great respect for people of the cloth; but the nun at St. Joe's was the one who didn't believe me. The Holy Spirit anoints certain people, but He wants us all to have His anointing. He wants each of us to have the things He has planned for us, yet certain legalistic religions don't allow that. Those religions have to let go of the legalism and make Jesus their Savior. It is written that they need to do this. I thought about that because I remembered how I'd accepted Jesus at 23 when I had made Him my Savior but didn't make Him my Lord. It was like He was telling me at that point when I gave birth that "I have something for you to do, my dear." I knew it, but I didn't know to what extent.

Even after that wonderful visitation, I still didn't get back into a born-again church. I'd go for a while but then return to my roots. I went hither and dither, back and forth—just floating. I know now that it was Satan's way of not letting me go forward, and I allowed it to happen because I didn't know how to take authority over my life. I did not know how to kick Satan out. I did not know how he was tormenting me, and he kept doing that a large share of the time when I had to raised my children alone.

Such a struggle! For self preservation, I pretended and learned early how to laugh everything off. I still giggle a lot, but now I have the joy of the Lord in my life since He has delivered me from a lot of things. At 28 I was still not delivered, and I know now the Lord was waiting for me. He never left me. I left Him.

I kept trying to raise my boys. My entire young years were spent raising them. Resentment built inside me due to the fact that I had to do it myself. Since I was flying to support us, I commuted from Warren to Cleveland at 4 a.m. so that I could start flying international flights all over the world—Honolulu, Japan, Germany, Paris. I flew on weekends, so I wasn't gone from my sons too long. Trying to juggle everything was getting to be too much.

On a flight one day I could not understand what a person was asking me, and all he wanted was a glass of water. I didn't feel connected, as if I wasn't even there. Surely something was seriously wrong with me. I spoke to one of my co-workers who suggested I get a check up. After going through a round of doctors and dentists, someone finally suggested that I see a psychologist whose explanation was, "You're exhausted from trying to handle everything on your own." My mind was shutting down from overload. He said that he could help me, but I never really felt right. His help was like a quick fix, not a long-term solution. I even took some nerve pills. When I did get better, I'm sure it's because I took some time off and rested.

After that, my physical problems began. I had uncontrollable diarrhea for over two months. My body parts kept breaking down. Stress! All I really ever needed to do was call on the Lord and be with Him. I was fighting it. I know that now, but I didn't then.

I was still trying to maintain a couple of relationships because I thought I just couldn't be alone. Marriage proposals came a couple of times. But as soon as I reached a certain point, I couldn't commit myself to anyone. I'd made mistakes. No way was I going to make another one! I decided I had to continue to do it all on my own. My independent spirit took over. It got into high gear and thought, "I can do this by myself! I don't need these doctors, or the men I'm dating, or anyone for that matter!" So I worked myself to the bone. I worked and came home and worked — kept a perfect house, made dinner, and tried to make a normal life for my boys. It got so bad commuting early in the morning from Warren to Cleveland that I ended up moving there. I still did not get into a born-again church, but I was seeking God. "God, how come this isn't working? I do love You. I don't understand. Why am I running into all of these road blocks?" As soon as I'd get on my feet and buy a place, something would happen with the boys or my job of flying. It just never seemed to quit.

The point is—I was still trying to control my own life. I couldn't give in. My father passed away, and my Mom was still living. I thought I could do it all. Mom raised me to be independent, and it is good to be that way. It is not good not to lean on the Lord because He will set you free from everything. I know that now because I have been through the maze of confusion, and I'm over it. I'm healed! Jesus healed me, and the rest of my story shows how He healed me.

After all of this mess, the boys got older and the problems got worse. They were out of control from the start of their teenage years. I asked my ex-husband to please take the boys for the summer to help out while I worked. He said, "No way. My wife will divorce me if you deposit the boys on my doorstep." I was desperate for some relief because I'd gone through enough. I can just imagine how young single women who haven't had the income, or the Mom, or the opportunities that I've had, must struggle. It was hard. I had to put bread on the table and do everything else besides. Financial support was meager and there were other problems. For example, babysitters stole from me, and one even tried to choke my son. Thank God, my mother was there to stop this and God protected my children from harm. Through it all I tried my best to keep a stable home. We wore our happy faces, but they were fake. Hurting inside and so upset with my life, I kept wondering how I was going to keep on doing everything.

When the boys reached the ages of 18 and 19, my household was totally out of control. (To understand the time frame — they are now 20 and 22, so this wasn't very long ago.) My oldest one had a break-up with a girlfriend and got into drugs. I think my youngest tried them too. Their personalities changed. I knew what was going on and tried to find them help, but found none.

Not able to figure out how to help them on my own, I even went to a hospital near where we lived and asked them to commit me. I told them, "I'm losing my mind." My children were driving me bonkers. I was coming home from trips to a house that was in total disarray. They never had parties there. On that one score they did go along with my wishes, but they showed no respect left for their mother at all. Their attitudes and grades were terrible. When they graduated, the principal told me, "You should get an award for what you've had to put up with just to get them through school." My boys weren't the hoodlum type. They dressed well and were good-looking young men. They just had no direction and I didn't either. I still loved the Lord and always said, "I know God will get us through," but it just wasn't happening.

A healing service was being held at a church in Cleveland, and a couple of friends asked me to attend. I went although I didn't know what to expect. I wondered what they did there. All I knew was that I needed to go somewhere for help. At my literal end, I wanted to pack my bags and leave the boys. I was that angry with them. I wanted to say, "Hey, I've fed and clothed you. I'm single and I raised you - yet you treat me like this after all I have done for you!" No matter what I did, they refused to obey me. Life really was intolerable. My own sons sometimes screamed obscenities at me in the street. Absolutely no respect. Control was gone.

At the healing service in that Catholic church, I sat down and waited. Praise God, I felt a sudden tingling from head to toe! I didn't know what an anointing was then, but I had a strange zinging all over. I'd come there with Rita, a dear sweet senior citizen friend of mine, and another lady. They began talking to the people seated next to them and didn't seem to be aware of or feeling anything. Neither woman appeared to have a clue as to what I was experiencing when I tried to tell them. I called it a "tingling sensation" for a long time since I had no idea what an anointing was.

That night the tingling never stopped. When the speaker came out and told of how Jesus had changed her life and how she wanted to pray for all of us, I went forward for prayer. I hadn't gone to the altar in years. Warren was the last I could remember. Trying to be independent, I had always tried to convince myself that I didn't need help. But I went then. No sooner had she put her hands on me, then I felt the tingling sensation go through my body even stronger than before. I fell softly to the floor. I couldn't get up for a long time. Finally I rose and went back to the pew

The women I'd come with were already in the car waiting for me. That chilly November night, I went to look for them but then went back inside to just sit in the presence of the Lord. I couldn't believe that they were in the car. They were gone, out of there, while I was having this incredible experience. God started to talk to me, "Charlene, you've got to give your heart to me. You've got to accept me into your heart. You've got to make me your Lord and Savior. You can't be half-way into the world anymore. I have a gift I'm going to give you. But you have to get yourself changed and I'm going to do it."

I started to cry and never stopped for perhaps an hour. The women were upset with me for taking so long, but that night I learned to listen to the Holy Spirit. Still, to this day, I listen. If you don't stop and tune into the Lord, how do you know when He has something He wants you to hear? You are going to miss it if you can't wait to get to the car and go home—you are going to miss out. It might take a while for the Holy Spirit to talk to you; but if you aren't listening, you won't hear. If you are talking all the time, He can't get in there. He talks to us, but we must learn to listen. That encounter with Him was six years ago. I'm still listening.

I had a difficult time in the car because the women were chattering. My desire was be alone. God had me and I needed to surrender to Him. I did. After that, I received so much more. Yes, things went wrong. The kids were still the same, but heat would pour from my hands and a tingling electricity would come from them. I went to my church in Cleveland and spoke to the priest. I asked him what he thought was going on. He said, "I don't know," but then he cautioned me not to "get crazy with this stuff." Next I went to a nun, Sister Mary Jane, and told her what was taking place. She believed me. She prayed for and with me.

Little by little, God started showing me His plans for my life. He'd wake me up in the middle of the night and give me scriptures in my ear—not my mind—my ear. I'd get up and go to the Bible and read. All of the scriptures had to do with Jesus' healing the sick and all of the miracles He performed. Every single time they were on healing. I knew something was coming because I felt different. The Lord was telling me to let go and not to try to be in control any more. I knew that He was going to give me a special thing to do. I wasn't sure how long it would take, so I started writing down insight from Him. He told me, "You will minister to thousands of people. You will lay your hands on them, and I will do the rest. You are not to do anything more than pray for them and, Charlene, I want you to use your hands. They are going to burn very hot and people will feel it. Some eyes will see—some will not; some ears will hear —some will not; some will be healed—and some will not."

He told me that early on, and I realized that tingling was anointing only after a Christian's explanation. I didn't read about it. The Lord had to teach me how He wanted. I told Him, "If this is truly from you, Lord, then teach me how to do what You want me to do, and I will be Your humble servant."

Looking back, I thought of how I was given a word by a man named Carlton Pearston years and years ago. While going through my divorce, I'd gone to Grace Church in Warren where he said that he had a "prophetic word." I wasn't sure I believed that, so I sat in the back seats and didn't go forward for prayer. I remember asking the Lord, "If this is for real and if You have something for me, let the speaker seek me out. I no more than said that when Carlton pointed his finger at me and said, "You! You don't know why you're going through the things you're going through. But you're going to help other people. God is going to give you the words to say and when not to say them." I don't recall all that he said, but nothing was mentioned about healing at that time, only that there was going to be an anointing on my life.

All these little things and all of the people I came into contact with made a difference in my life. I met Dr. Robert Schuller in Denver, CO, while he was eating an ice cream cone. He asked me a few questions and I answered them. Others questioned me. I know now that God was wanting to do a work in me.

My life was pretty messed up. Everything was not in place. Not only my mind and heart weren't right, but my condo needed to be fixed up too. I loved decorating. Whenever I got depressed, I painted. I lived there 10 years and had the kitchen 4 different colors. I painted and papered when I didn't know what else to do. I also was crazy about moving furniture, changing it at least once a week. The kids would leave in the morning, and I'd move a chair and they could wind up on the floor later. It was a family joke after a while. But it was obsessive, and my whole family was aware that I did this. I was trying to change my home, but it was me that needed changing. I was quite a gossiper at the time. I'd talk about my friends saying things like, "She doesn't wear the right dresses," or "her hair's a mess." I swore and drank. For a while I smoked but was delivered from that. I was just not walking with the Lord. The men in my life weren't right either. I needed to change. I wasn't going to find Jesus in these men. They were spending money on me, and I didn't want them to; but if they didn't, I got mad at them. I was such a shallow person.

I kept on smiling and laughing and had everyone thinking that things were just fine. Yet on the inside, I was a mess. I needed a cure. A big one. When I started changing was when God started really working. Remember: He gave me the anointing, then He changed me. He gave me the physical feeling of what His love is a few times. He always gave me His love. It was just that I wasn't ready to accept it.

One day a painter was painting my bathroom when a friend of mine called and asked for a document, which was a proxy for the United Airlines meeting she was attending. She didn't have hers and needed mine. I told her, "Come on over and get it." As I hung up the phone, I realized that as I had been cleaning out drawers I might have thrown it away. I'd taken three garbage bags out on to the patio. I mentioned to the painter, I'll call him Joe, that I might have thrown the paper out. He said, "Go through the garbage." When he spoke it was as if Jesus had spoken a directive from God to go through the garbage - NOW! I felt God was using that man to tell me what to do. God does use people around us, the ones we don't even think are going to help us in life. They might not even realize that they have helped, but they do because God uses them.

As I went through the first bag, I had to sift through pork chop bones, kitty litter, and a whole mess of other disgusting things. I felt repulsed - physically ill. I asked myself, "Can I really be doing this?" Not finding the paper, I closed the bag and returned it to the patio. When I told 'Joe' that I hadn't found it, he said, "Go through the next bag." Another directive. An order. I somehow sensed that God was speaking to me, and I got that bag out and went through it. More garbage.

All of a sudden I felt His anointing while I'm sorting through discarded waste! At the bottom I still didn't find the paper, but I began mentally getting rid of things—anxiety, hurts, anger. After that, Joe said, "Go through the last bag and you'll find it." As I did, I began crying and carrying on because I knew God was saying, "Charlene, you have to get out of the garbage. You have to throw it away. Give it back. You can't carry this on your shoulders anymore. Yes, you have made a ton of mistakes; you have made the wrong choices in men. No, you haven't done the right things sometimes, but you are my child and I love you. I want you to be freed of all these things."

I realized what was taking place as I finished the last bag, and a sense of spiritual uplifting and humbleness swept over me. Humbleness in how God has changed me - not just those few times - but how He has been changing me all of my life. When I got rid of the garbage, a light bulb went off — in my mind. God showed me that the paper was in the back seat of the car. I went out to the car. The paper was on the back seat! I got it and my friend came to pick it up, totally unaware of what had happened to me. But I had this new anointing, and I knew I had to give up everything and surrender to God.

Soon after that, God said, "I want to use you now." He taught me how to be humble and how to surrender. Then he taught me how to receive His healing. Such a wonderful experience! As a flight attendant, I didn't use my healing in flight for a long time, but God walked me through. I was able to pray for people in K-Mart, a shoe store, or wherever He brought people to me. The first or second person I prayed for God reminded me that some eyes would see - some would not; some would hear - some would not; and some would be healed - and some would not.

At that time when I wasn't preaching salvation as I am now, I met a man at a meat counter. He looked at me. I looked at him. He said he was hurting inside and began to tell me his life story. I asked, "Why are you telling me this?" He said, "I don't know." I told him, " I know - it's the Holy Spirit." I ended up going to his place to pray with him. He was slain in the spirit in his chair with joy and happiness on his face.

Numerous healings have taken place since that day. Many people have come to the Lord. For a number of years now, when I'm flying, God has brought people from all over the world to me. On a flight one day the pilot was complaining about his ear aching, something that could keep him distracted from his job. As the burning sensation came into my left hand, I placed it on his ear. "The pain is gone!" he cried, and he asked me, "How did you do that?" "I didn't," I replied, "Jesus did!" I praise God because I'm just His vessel and the True Healer is Jesus Christ. Once I'd made Him my Lord and Savior, He gave this gift to me, but I didn't understand it. I was blinded and had fear. He said, *"For God has not given us the spirit of fear; but of power and of a sound mind."* When I found that scripture in II Timothy 1:7 (KJV), I knew my fear would be lifted and that I could take authority over the devil in Jesus' name.

Then Satan could no longer torment me like he did Job. Back in the hospital when I was first given the anointing of the Holy Spirit with His love, He told me to read Job in the Bible. I didn't understand then how Satan could come in and deteriorate me at my weakest point, as he does to all of us if we let Him. Even after I went through anxiety and depression, — I've been healed of so many things that I can't even talk about. God will heal you. I just praise God today that I can help or touch someone else and let Jesus' power heal them, their broken hearts, alone-times, little children suffering from incest, abusers. Often women who have had abortions think God doesn't love them. He loves us all. People who think they are not worthy, God will give another chance—a second, third, and even a fourth one. You just need to come to Him. I don't mean to preach, but I want you to know what God is doing in my life. I wouldn't want it any other way. Make Jesus your Lord and Savior, surrender to His Holy Spirit, and let Him guide you. Don't try to do it yourself like I did. I was in control for many years. It just didn't work.

The Lord has even healed me from my fear of being hurt in my relationship with men. When I went back to live near Youngstown, I met a man I'd known even before my airline career. After that, we both went our separate ways. When we met again, Jerry and I had a new love—the love of the Lord between us. Our love grew. Two years went by, but I feared a commitment to any male, even though I'd agreed to become engaged to this wonderful man. One evening we attended a Crossing Paths meeting and had a word spoken to us: "I was to get over the fear," and "Jerry was to get over the hurt." "Hurt?" I realized then that every time my dear fiancee suggested marriage, I thought of some excuse not to become his wife. Of course he was hurt!

That night we each experienced a healing. We both knew the Lord wanted us to be man and wife. We set the date in October and gathered friends and relatives to witness our merger. That date will always be cherished by both of us. Jerry has a son who had been missing his mother ever since her death. My two handsome offspring were there along with Jerry's boy, Jon. How proud we were to see the three of them sitting together in the pew.

My heart nearly burst as my Wayne got up and gave a

speech about our lives and how the Lord had changed them, especially his own. He told of exchanging drugs for Jesus at a Promise Keepers meeting several years ago. Jesus is the Healer! Our lives, including my dear Mother's, have become so much richer. Eric still needs to find the Lord, but I love him so much that I'll pray him into the Kingdom.

When I became Mrs. Jerry Pasko, I knew the Lord was pleased with the marriage. Jesus had equipped me with a healing ministry, and now I have a husband who backs me all the way.

Jerry and Charlene have both been touched by the Master, and they know the things He's done for them, He'll do for you if you ask Him into YOUR heart!

* * * * *

Charlene and Jerry can be reached at Second Chance Ministries, 1714 Boardman-Poland Rd. # 11, Poland, Oh 44514. Tel. 330-707-0306 or 330-757-8089.

Crossing Paths Treasury Offered On Tape!

A first for us! So many people seem to like to listen to tapes that Son-Rise will offer, for the first time ever, a taped version of this book!

Two 95 minute tapes packaged in an album set
Only $14.95

Two 95 minute tapes packaged in a box set
Only $9.95

Order yours today - great for gift giving!!

Other books and products from Son-Rise

Devotionals
Penned from the Heart - Vol. III $9.95
Penned from the Heart - Vol. IV $9.95
Penned from the Heart - Vol. V $9.95

The Amish Eden Series
Dawn of Eden $9.95
Search for Eden $9.95
Return to Eden $9.95
Beyond Eden $9.95

Historical Series
Dog Jack $9.95
Daughter of the Dawn $9.95
For the Love of Adam $9.95
Singing Cowboy $9.95

Biographies
Now I'll Bet On You Lord $7.95
  (Don Reed's complete story)
But God Knew - Ann Thomas $7.95

Poetry
Sweet Inspirations - Marsha Kamovitch $5.95
Time to Live - Andy Stallsmith $5.95

Special Message
Moffat the Prophet $5.95
Crafted with Love $5.95

Nutrition
Green Supreme™ with Barley Power
200 Tablets of Green Barley $14.99
200 Tablets of Green Barley with Cayenne $14.99
150 Tablets of Green Barley with
  Chromium Picolinate $14.99

For ordering or more information please call
1-800-358-0777